I0820086

FRANCO PEPE

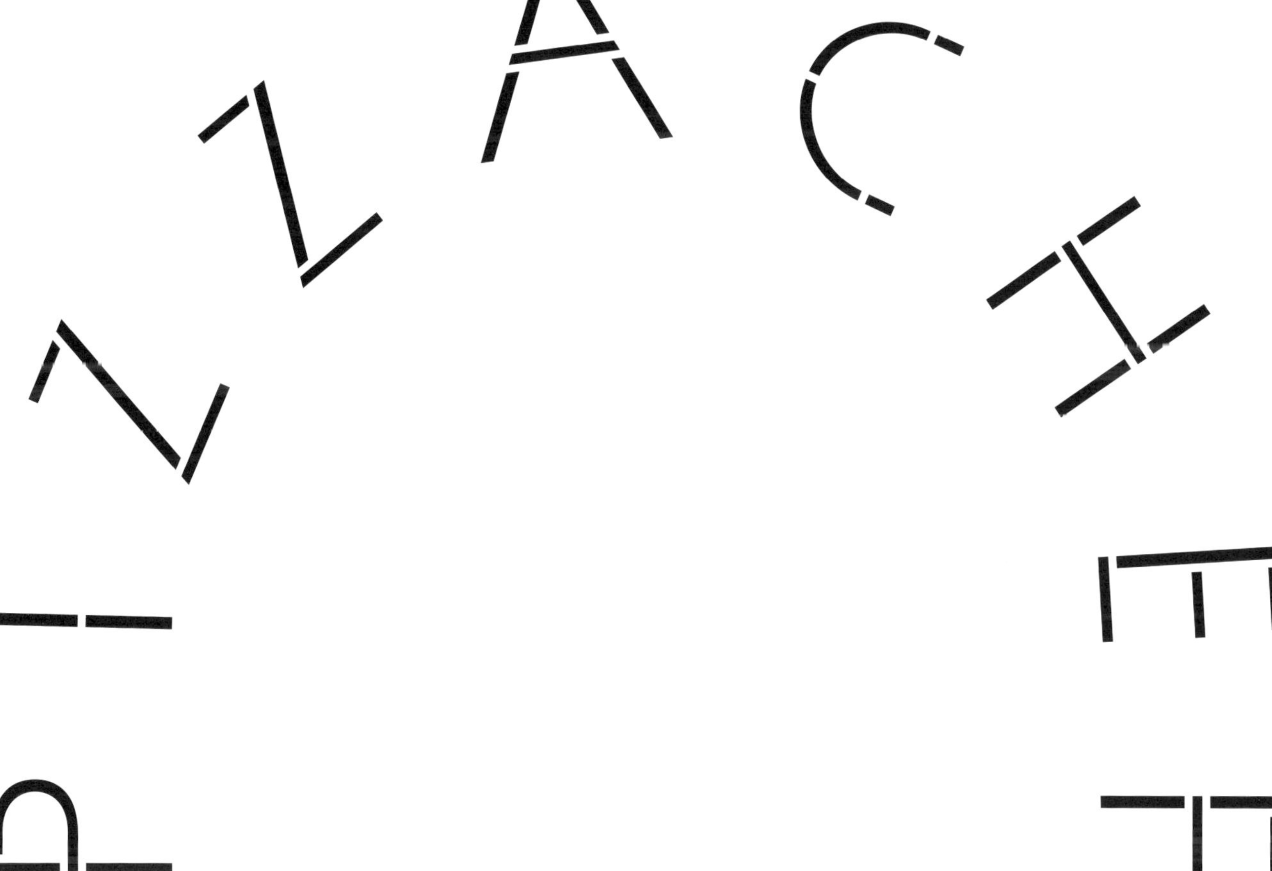

FRANCO PEPE

Text by
Elisia Menduni

Photography by
Adam Bricker and Brian McGinn

Faith Willinger

I met Franco Pepe for the first time in Milan in 2012. He did a presentation at Identità Golose, going into detail about his pizza philosophy, demonstrating technique, offering a taste. I was already a pizza fanatic, having previously learned the art from Neapolitan master Enzo Coccia at a private lesson he gave for Japanese chefs. Franco's pizza amazed. The crust was light, airy, the topping delicious, perfectly balanced. I was impressed; it was love at first bite. I spoke to him afterward, he was kind, and I promised to visit.

I soon made a pilgrimage to the unremarkable village of Caiazzo to watch Franco in action at his pizzeria. He was obsessed with ingredients, and knew his producers well. Flour, tomatoes, mozzarella, extra virgin oil, all carefully chosen, all local. Most *pizzaioli* used commercial flour, but not Franco. And everyone else made dough in stainless steel mixers, slapped by dough hooks, but not Franco. His dough, treated with respect, was kneaded by hand in a wooden box called a *madia*, allowing him to constantly feel almost imperceptible changes of this most important ingredient. It was like the difference between pasta hand-rolled on a wooden board with a wooden pin instead of smashed between stainless steel rollers. The warmth of wood instead of cool steel, the heat of his hands, all contributed to his extraordinary product. Franco was truly in touch with his dough. He was also concerned with health, conferring with doctors and professors who explained the digestive process and nutritional values of his pizza. He wore a medical mask, since breathing flour in the air wasn't healthy. I named him Doctor Dough.

My friend Brian McGinn, *Chef's Table* creator-producer who I bonded with while filming Corrado Assenza's episode for the pastry series, was as obsessed with pizza as I was. When he learned that I was planning a return to Pepe in Grani to spend time with Franco, he asked if he could join me. He was as inspired as I was and proposed a *Chef's Table* series about pizza, telling the stories of *pizzaioli* from all over the world. Of course Brian directed Franco's episode. The world arrived in Caiazzo to experience his sublime pizza. And pizza and *pizzaioli* are now treated with respect.

Nancy Silverton

Twelve years ago, Faith Willinger, the self-proclaimed "born again Italian" food writer, told me and my partner Michael we needed to go to the small town of Caiazzo in Campania to have the pizza of Franco Pepe, who I had never heard of. Well, it wasn't that she "told" us to go, but rather she "ordered" us to go.

"If you want to have the best pizza in Italy then you must go to Franco Pepe's in Caiazzo near Caserta," Faith ordered.

Following orders was never so delicious.

We walked down the narrow cobblestone path that leads to "Pepe in Grani" and into the charming pizzeria, and were seated at a warm outside table beneath the stars. Our expectations were as sky high as those stars. Franco Pepe's pizzas soared beyond those stars.

The particular pizza that stole our hearts is called "Il sole nel piatto," also known, to us (and Franco) alone, as "The Dream of Caiazzo." We had asked a delightful female server what her favorite pizza was and we thought she said that "Il sole nel piatto" was "my dream."

Since then, Franco Pepe's pizzas have been my dream. The other day I wondered, if I had eaten a pizza from Franco Pepe before I opened my pizzeria, would I have ever opened my pizzeria?

What sets Pepe in Grani apart is the brilliant quality of the stuff on top of that hand-mixed, hand-stretched dough. Even the basil. You bite into it and it's like saying "Yes, I'm basil! And proud of it." Same thing with the anchovies, the olives, the tomatoes, the bufala mozzarella—all of impeccable quality.

At my home in Los Angeles, I rarely dine west of La Cienega Boulevard, which is about six miles away. But, during the summer, at my place in Umbria, if someone suggested we go to get a pizza from Franco Pepe in Caiazzo, which is 211 miles away, I would simply say "Let's go."

Daniel Young

On December 2023 I returned to Pepe in Grani, the pizza restaurant in the hilltop village of Caiazzo, to wrong-foot the world's most acclaimed pizza maker.

I've been on first-name terms with Franco Pepe from the get-go. It's the proper etiquette: you pick up a slice of Franco's pizza (not Franco *Pepe*'s pizza) with your hands, to let its warmth and softness get a hold on you. World-class though it may be, it's still pizza. It's a first-name pleasure, very informal.

With a level of accomplishment matched in intensity by his unwavering sense of purpose, Franco has reshaped a craft, in his own first name.

On the hour's drive up from Naples I rehearsed in my head the confession I would deliver to Franco prior to a pizza-tasting dinner.

I was to remind him just how much I was dazzled by his signature pizza, the Sbagliata, when I first tried it in London in 2015 at his pizza pop-up at Harrods department store. His reconstruction of the Margherita was encrypted as if in Morse code, with green dots of basil purée and red dashes of tomato.

It looked childlike in its simplicity, except—trust me—squeeze-bottle decoration is a lot more difficult to get right than it appears. If the Hungarian painter, photographer, and writer László Moholy-Nagy had created a Bauhaus pizza, it might have resembled the Sbagliata. Only then would the naysayers of the 1920s have insisted any six-year-old could have made that pizza.

I faulted the Sbagliata only in relation to the off-menu Margherita Franco prepared for me in 2017 at Pepe in Grani, in his father's style. Forget avant-garde; Stefano Pepe's Margherita was an old-school pizza in all respects except one: he sprinkled it with the local oregano he gathered in the Matese foothills.

Then, as today, the green in the *tricolore* of the classic, Neapolitan-style Margherita was always provided by fresh basil, never, heaven forbid, oregano.

That whiff of oregano reminded me of the pizzas I had with my family back in the day, back home in New York. The pizza makers at New York's Italian restaurants and sit-down pizzerias reached first for dried oregano, not fresh basil, for their so-called cheese pizzas. I don't remember any of them using the term Margherita prior to 1975.

With Franco, my intended destination was not New York. I hoped my provocation, such as it was, would take us instead to the front line of a debate simmering in pizzeria kitchens, dining areas, and discussion forums. Any comparison of the new and old Margheritas would raise the tradition-vs-innovation question, and thereby echo a proverbial conflict that mystifies the New World as it haunts the old one. In southern Italy it's like dark espresso: you drink it every morning and channel the caffeine and bitterness into the generational struggle for—or against—incremental change.

Franco saw things differently. That's part of what makes him Franco. He did not view the comparison I had raised as one representative of any eternal conflict between preservation and transformation. Much as we rebel against our parents, we discover in later years we have more in common with them than we imagine. Only very recently did Franco make this connection: His father the *pizzaiolo* rebelled, in his own way, against Neapolitan pizza dictates. He was a farm-to-*forno* forager, decades before *locavore* became a culinary buzzword.

"We interpreted our territory," recalls Franco. "My father added the scent of Matese oregano to his Margherita. I reimagined mine with the local *pomodoro riccio* and created the Margherita Sbagliata. Both Margheritas were born from the same will to love the land."

A decade ago, the inventive Greek chef Christoforos Peskias made the following admission. Every day his goal was to create a modern dish equal to and possibly even superior to the timeless "horiatiki" salad, though deep down he understood that this was a futile endeavor. No matter the modern miracles he performed with feta powder or tomato foam, there was no improving upon a classic as basic and perfect as a country-style Greek salad seasoned with salt, extra virgin olive oil, and dried oregano.

I imagined Franco feeling the same way about his dad's Margherita. Despite his heroic efforts to invent a pizza superior to his father's version, did he secretly know the objective that possibly motivated him was unattainable?

"That's what I've always said," Franco acknowledged. "When innovation is grounded in simplicity it's hard to raise the bar." Those words from the most influential pizza maker of our time may sound like they're coming from a chef rather than a *pizzaiolo*. It's a distinction that matters to pizza professionals who scoff at assertions that Franco is in a class of his own. "Franco Pepe is not a *pizzaiolo*," confides the pizza flour king of Naples. "He's a chef."

"Franco Pepe is not a Neapolitan *pizzaiolo*," whispers a mouthpiece for the Naples pizza police.

The dismissive words are intended, I suspect, as a subtle put-down, echoing, inciting, upholding, or inflaming disparaging views in the pizza community.

But even if such gossip swayed opinion against Franco, I doubt its intended target would mind if he overheard these particular comments. Or if initially enraged, not so much by the content but rather by the intent of these offhand remarks, Franco would cool down within hours.

Firstly, his heroes are chefs, not *pizzaioli*. He turns to Michelin-starred chefs for ideas, motivation, and approbation. When creating a new pizza he thinks like a chef. I picture him in the driver's seat of his Audi Q5, looking into the windshield and imagining a sketchbook where he can evaluate new associations of ingredients or rethink classic combinations.

Secondly, Franco does not see himself as a Neapolitan *pizzaiolo*, even if a slice of the pizza world outside Italy does. It's true, he did grow up around Caiazzo, some 50 kilometres north of Naples, the holy city of pizza. And his soft-crusted pizza does have much more in common with classic Neapolitan pizza than, say, New York pizza, Roman pizza, or other regional styles.

But Franco's territory in the southern Italian region of Campania is the province of Caserta, not The Metropolitan City of Naples. With Pepe in Grani he established himself as a founding father of two global pizza movements: personal pizza and local pizza. The first is a self-portrait of the pizza maker; the second, a portrayal of his terroir.

Ambitious young pizza makers all over the world turn to these depictions of the pizza heartland for inspiration. Reinterpretations of the Sbagliata abound, much to Franco's delight. To the extent that there is an argument, he's won it.

Franco fits his pizza innovations into several formats and shapes, among them classic, *in ruoto* (a fluffier pan pizza), and deep-fried cones. Differences in texture and composition are determined by the shaping and cooking of the pizza base. Each is made with the same dough, mixed by hand to Franco's strict specifications.

"What's most beautiful about this dough is its versatility," says Franco. "Each expression evokes a different emotion on the palate.

“The identity of a *pizzaiolo* is his dough. I must show you only one dough so that you know Franco the *pizzaiolo*.”

So there you have it: Franco may think like a chef, but clearly he wants us to know he is a *pizzaiolo* who’s brought prestige to a traditionally humble profession. His pizza is still pizza. As good as anyone’s pizza, maybe even his father’s, only better.

Franco Pepe

Introduction

Mediterranean cuisine is far from unique in having water and wheat as its key staples. Over the centuries, the adoption of these two ingredients, with such magnificent accompaniments as olive oil and tomato, has created something truly delicious, a perfect balance of nutrients and flavor, seasoning, and substance.

The combination of wheat flour, water, and the surrounding environment has always been a source of life, fermented products, and yeasts, but it took several geological eras for humanity to begin to truly comprehend this. For thousands of years the simple act of kneading has created unexpected alchemies and extraordinary developments, and these in turn have led, over the centuries, to great achievements and innovations. It is through this magical process—dictated first of all by the simplicity of the ingredients, and then by numerous links between people, the environment, the soil, and human culture—that pizza has come to represent an absolute, eternal, and irreplaceable food within the field of international gastronomy and cuisine.

Over the last twenty years, in Italy and around the globe, pizza has enjoyed a history characterized by revolution, research, and exceptional innovation. As an anthropologist, I have always been interested in the ritual and sociological aspects of food. Even though this book is primarily a biography of a great pizza chef, and the story of one of the best pizzas in the world, it is important to remember that such an apparently simple and down-to-earth foodstuff is a crucial source of nutrition, with its origins in the deep past.

Thanks to recent findings in the Jordanian Black Desert, we know that bread is the oldest surviving food in human history. Archaeological excavations in 2018 at the site of Shubayqa (in northern Jordan) uncovered the remains of a baking area, very similar to a pizza oven, fueled by wood, and with a central flat stone on which the dough was baked. Among the finds at Shubayqa was a kind of carbonized unleavened pizza made from pounded cereals, probably wild spelt and barley. This discovery is very important for the history of humanity: it is proof that about 14,000 years ago, in the heart of the Fertile Crescent—long before the emergence and spread of agriculture—someone cooked an ancestral food made of wheat. Some prehistorians have even suggested that it was precisely this very early pizza-style bread that led to the development of sedentary populations in Mesopotamia and triggered the beginnings of agriculture.

Pizza is a popular, fun, and universal food. Essentially a cheap street food, it has adapted successfully to each different culture into which it has been introduced, mainly by Italian immigrants as they have moved around the world. Wherever it has landed, pizza has reinvented itself, resulting not only in unusual local variations, but also in fierce battles concerning its origins that today form the themes of conferences, awards, guides, and books.

Franco Pepe and I first met in 2011. Together with Stefano Bonilli, founder of the *Gambero Rosso* magazine and a great Italian journalist and food critic, we were organizing the A' Pizza event on the Neapolitan coast. Today there are many events celebrating pizza, but back then this occasion was a bit of a "black swan" on the Italian food and wine scene, and the first attempt to launch pizza as a high-quality, prestige gastronomic product.

With the A' Pizza event not far from Vico, in Costiera, we wanted to talk not only about Neapolitan pizza, but about Italian pizza as a whole; to represent the full national spectrum of pizza styles, while mapping out the fascinating evolution of the sector in recent decades. The choice of Italian pizza chefs was not difficult, because at the time those responsible for quality, pioneering work in Italy could be counted on the fingers of one hand; it nevertheless took us over a month to choose between the Neapolitan chefs and those of the rest of Campania.

Alongside Bonilli and some friends from Campania, we set out to make a dedicated map of the universe of Neapolitan pizza. Working our way through endless lists of pizzerias in Naples and the surrounding region was distinctly problematic. It was no easy task to find impartial guides to lead us through this chaos, like Virgil through Dante's Inferno. Before going to the capital of Campania, we collected articles and listened to opinions for months. Then, with the help of our advisors, we spent several weeks in and around Naples, sampling many different pizzas and personally checking out doughs, ingredients, styles, and above all the stories and passions of great pizza artisans.

In 2005 Carla Capalbo, an American journalist and author of fascinating gastronomic guides and cookbooks, published *The Food and Wine Guide to Naples and Campania*. She was the first to publicize many small businesses, producers, restaurants, and pizzerias in lesser-known regions, and I visited her at her home in the medieval hill town of Nusco, where she told me about the Campania pizza scene from the perspective of a New Yorker. An attentive reporter with an elegant descriptive style, Carla took me through the rich and complex world of Neapolitan pizza, presenting me with a picture of the political aspects of the sector, and the delicate balances that required full attention and reflection. Then, when the subject returned to a more down-to-earth, taste-oriented gastronomic level, I asked her which pizza she personally preferred. She said, "Elisia, if you can manage it, go to Caiazzo. It's a bit out of the way, but Franco Pepe's pizza is well worth the journey. His pizza is light and simple. It's sublime! Just go!" She was the first writer to speak internationally about this remote pizzeria in Caiazzo, and it was Carla who insisted that we include Antica Osteria Pizzeria Pepe in the list of pizzerias to visit for the A' Pizza event.

Our time in Naples was intense and beautiful. For us food journalists, who had perhaps been a little too focused on haute cuisine and "new" styles of cooking, the process of rediscovering the simplicity of such a basic food was a valuable life lesson. These were unforgettable days spent visiting mills and cheese producers, and tasting the best pizzas of my life. Then, on the last day of our research, after a few pit stops among the cheeseries of Caserta, we headed northwards on the Strada Provinciale 336, following the directions of Carla Capalbo, arriving at sunset in the main square of Caiazzo. The Antica Osteria Pizzeria Pepe was located in Piazza Porta Vetere, opposite the park. Franco Pepe welcomed us and began to tell us the story of his family, of his father Stefano's pizza, and of the beauty of the area. Despite the many kilos of carbs and dairy products that we had already absorbed like slow, greedy snails during the itinerary of the previous days, the succession of tastings at Antica Osteria Pizzeria Pepe did not weigh us down. Of all the pizzas we tasted, I was particularly struck by the Endive Calzone. The crunchiness of the leaves, the lightness of the dough, and the contrasting bitterness of the small Caiatina olives, was unforgettable. I had never tasted anything so good. Every individual flavor was distinct, everything was balanced, and the delicacy of the dough in the upper dome of the Calzone was incredible.

What makes Franco Pepe unique is his fresh vision of the world of pizza—the desire, at first instinctive, and then built with meticulous care, to create a new kind of pizza that is deeply distinctive, capable of preserving all the fundamental elements of its roots in the past, but also looking with eager eyes to the future. A pizza kneaded by hand for three generations, which instead of being based on recipes and technique, is based on the sensitivity of people, on the senses—sight, smell, and above all touch. The hands perceive the state of a dough, feel the temperature, and understand how the flour absorbs water, salt, and yeast, how it develops and rises, and how it reaches equilibrium: the "dough point." The timings and quantities of ingredients in the recipe change according to the humidity, climate, seasons, and temperatures. Sometimes they may even depend on the mood of the person kneading. The techniques, however, remain constant, and are the same as those of Franco's father Stefano, and his grandfather Francesco. To the incredible legacy of family tradition that Franco received, this pizza chef from Caiazzo has added research, commitment, and an unparalleled passion. Now owner of Pepe in Grani, his pizza is made with ingredients from the local area, prepared with techniques that are both traditional and highly innovative, and inspired by visits to the kitchens of great Italian chefs. This mix of the new and the old makes every pizza an absolute delight.

CASERTA 20
CAIAZZO 5
PIEDIMONTE M. 14
ALVIGNANO 4

TERRITORY

19

The »Other« Campania

Franco Pepe was born in Caiazzo, the city of his parents and grandparents. For anyone arriving from the capital or any other metropolis, it may seem strange to describe Caiazzo as a "city." To those accustomed to wide avenues and heavy traffic, it seems more like a village, a peaceful and quiet collection of houses accompanied by a castle, perched on the top of a hill overlooking the Volturno Valley. Its many small alleyways descend like capillaries from the main artery, the Corso, which follows the path of the classic Roman *decumanus* (the east–west road in a Roman military camp). However, Caiazzo was founded as a real city, built by the Opici as a defensive stronghold on the top of a hill to the right of the Volturno river, from which they controlled the plains north of the Tifatini mountains and beyond.

As an Etruscan, Samnite, and later Roman city, Caiazzo had an important role to play thanks to its key position along the Appian Way, the ancient Roman road that connected Rome with Brundisium (now Brindisi), and considered by the Romans themselves to be the "Queen of Roads." Before the year 1000 CE, Caiazzo was a diocese, a feudal seat (in fact a feudal state), and finally a bishopric.

With the fall of the Western Roman Empire, Caiazzo suffered barbarian incursions, but continued to be a vital center during the early Middle Ages. Over the centuries, the city came under the control of various rulers, including the Lombards, the Normans, the Swabians, and the Angevins; each ruler left their mark, contributing to the creation of the rich historical and cultural mosaic of the city.

For centuries, historians confused Caiazzo with Calatia (now Maddaloni, a municipality not far from Caserta). Then, at the end of the nineteenth century, the German historian Theodor Mommsen used ancient coins and inscriptions (the Corpus Inscriptionum Latinarum) to establish definitively that the modern city of Caiazzo was ancient Caiatia, not Calatia. This strange tendency to repeatedly fail to recognize the true identity of Caiazzo has been a constant in the history of the city. Even during the Second World War, Caiazzo was subject to bombing because it was confused with one of the inhabited centers near Cassino. Due to this tragic error, on January 27, 1944 the US planes, instead of attacking the Germans as they retreated from the Monastery of Cassino, hit Caiazzo instead, killing many civilians.

The alleyways of Caiazzo.

A small tabernacle with the Virgin Mary on the terrace
at the Agriturismo Le Campestre.
Pages 24–25: The landscape of Caiazzo.

Today, the elegant mansions lining the main street evoke the centuries during which Caiazzo was one of the principal cities of the Upper Caserta area, and every part of the city is typical of many of the towns of Samnium, the ancient territory located between Lazio, Molise, Abruzzo, and Campania. This is a small city, rich in history, where you can lose yourself among stone alleyways, ancient houses with terraces packed with citrus trees, and views of the beautiful valley below.

To understand Franco Pepe—in particular the combative nature of this unique pizza chef—it is useful to understand his own region and history, beyond Caiazzo, avoiding the stereotypes and generalizations that often lump everything together. It is all too easy for a rich and varied region like Campania to be known only for Vesuvius, Pompeii, the Amalfi coast, pizza, and the alleys of Naples. In reality, there are many Campanias: the great metropolis at the foot of Vesuvius, the coasts and the islands, the Bourbon palaces, and the Greek temples. And then there is inland Campania, less well-known and less frequented, with its shepherds and mountaineers, fewer highways and more sheep tracks, and a different, more sober sense of life, which must be respected and shared, unless you prefer to pack your bags and head towards Naples or the north.

The history of this territory is also a tale of many peoples. Its roots predate the Roman conquest and Campania's formal integration (but not complete absorption) into what would become a great empire. Some of these peoples have always been here, while others have arrived at various times into wonderful, fertile territory, with copious agriculture, livestock, and commercial opportunities.

The Greeks came first, naming their newly founded capital Neapolis ("new city"), later abbreviated to Naples. This refined and cultured maritime port not only looked towards Greece but also recalled the myths of Egypt. Then came the Etruscans, whose origins remain controversial, and who established a good understanding with the Greeks, happily exchanging trade, customs, and divinities. Clear traces of this intense Etruscan presence can be found to the north and south of Vesuvius, and have also emerged from the excavations of Pompeii and Herculaneum.

The Samnites, on the other hand, had inhabited Campania (as well as Molise and Abruzzo) since time immemorial, and their culture was characterized by a marked territoriality. They were essentially mountaineers and warriors, well adapted to this particularly rugged section of the Apennine range, and ready to wield their weapons with the same disciplined vigor with which they used agricultural tools. The Samnites represented a significant obstacle to the expansion of the Romans, and it took three military campaigns to subdue them. There were many

incidents along the way, including the Battle of the Caudine Forks, which tells us all we need to know about the stubbornness of the Samnites. The year was 321 BCE, and the Roman army was trapped in a gorge, with the only two exits blocked by the Samnites. The Romans understood that surrender was the only option, but the Samnites chose to humiliate their enemies, making them pass under a yoke, unarmed and half-naked, surrounded by insults and mockery. Taking this on the chin, the Romans recovered and ultimately defeated the Samnites, and from 290 BCE onwards the Samnites were subjugated by Rome.

Mount Vesuvius at sunset, as seen from the Sorrento Coast, across the Bay of Naples.

The bellicose, imperialistic aspects of the Romans were always balanced by a zest for life and a constant search for pleasure: in Campania this meant looking for thermal springs and constructing wonderful villas where they could enjoy the naturally heated water (think of the spas at Ischia, Agnano, and Fuorigrotta). The Romans were also providers of entertainment, building theaters everywhere (including the beautiful examples at Benevento, Naples, Sessa Aurunca, Acerra, Teano, Herculaneum, and Pompeii) and creating huge amphitheaters for their gladiatorial shows (at Cuma, Santa Maria Capua Vetere, Avella, Pozzuoli, and Pompeii, the latter producing Spartacus himself).

Today, the only surviving traces of the Samnites are walls and hilltop villages, the sparse but imposing remnants of their warrior nature. Always ready to attack and defend themselves from aggressors, they were nevertheless equally dedicated to grazing animals and cultivating their fields. To understand the Samnite territory, one must look north, taking in the white stone mountains of Matese and the uncontaminated beauty of centuries-old woods. It is here that we can search for the few archaeological fragments that are still visible today, such as the cyclopean walls of Caiazzo, the hilltop castles, and the fortified walls of places like Treglia. A small hamlet in the municipality of Pontelatone, near Mount Maggiore, Treglia was originally Trebula Baliniensis, the last independent center of the Samnites, which survived even after the three wars with the Romans. With its huge megalithic walls, amply withstanding the passage of time, and its entrance gate strongly recalling the Lion Gate at Mycenae, this is one of the few remaining symbols of the tough, impenetrable, diligent, and warlike culture of Samnium.

Our exploration of the upper Caserta area has taken us a long way from the Campania that most people think they know: the "fashionable" Campania that is to be seen in Naples, Capri, and the Amalfi coast. Culturally speaking, coastal Campania has very little in common with that mountainous, green, rugged, severe, and remote "other" Campania.

When Campania became part of the Roman political sphere, during the fourth and third centuries BCE, the beautiful villas of rich Roman senators began to be built throughout the region, attracted by such features as the charm of the sea, the uncontaminated nature of the fertile plain around Capua ("Campania Felix"), the beauty of the Gulf of Naples, and the richness of the thermal springs. Archaeological excavations in the region have revealed especially abundant traces of the "blessed life" enjoyed by many Romans in Campania. In Pompeii and Herculaneum, due to the dramatic eruption of Vesuvius in 79 CE, the evidence of these lives survives famously and vividly in the form of the very bodies of the people stricken suddenly by the torrent of volcanic rock and pumice, as well as in the frescoes and mosaics in their houses and villas. These representations of the reality of everyday life in the Roman era in Campania tell us a great deal about their lived experiences of pleasure, levity, music, theater, sex, wine, and lots of food.

Today, we can visit the intact preserved remains of inns and rotisseries of the time, full of original charm and details. In the *thermopolium* (fast-food counter) discovered at Pompeii in 2020, the two hanging ducks, fish, and many chickens painted on the walls give us the full menu of this incredible rotisserie from two thousand years ago. Also at Pompeii,

Left and opposite: Street scenes in Caiazzo.
Pages 30–31: Sunbathing on the rocks in Naples.

ASSOCIAZIONE
NAZIONALE
COMB. e REDUCI

a fresco inside a villa discovered in 2023 portrays *xenia* (gifts that the family gave to the gods), including fruit, a jug of wine, and a focaccia loaf, which many have interpreted as a direct ancestor of the pizza. This disk of dough enriched with pomegranates, dates, and walnuts is strongly reminiscent of the classic Neapolitan pizza.

The borders of Campania also tell the story of the disputed nature of the territory. The current administrative division between the Italian regions does not properly recognize the ancient human geography that originally marked out the borders—especially the cultural limits—of the Samnite lands. Modern Campania sits to the south of the Lazio and Molise regions, whereas Campania Felix (known in medieval times as Terra di Lavoro/"Land of Work") covered a wider area during the period from the Normans to the Swabians, from Napoleon to the Bourbons, right up to the formation of the kingdom of Italy. Fascism abolished the Terra di Lavoro, with Caserta as its capital, in 1927, and the modern province of Caserta was created as recently as 1947.

To understand the Alto Casertano region and the immediate territory of Caiazzo, it is important to understand these historical elements because they are tangible signs of the cultural distance between the Campania plain, which looks out onto the Gulf of Naples and the sea, and the Campania of the mountains and woods.

In all this geography, Naples is a world apart—isolated from everything else in its splendid anarchic individuality. Though we should not so much speak of Neapolitan isolation as of detachment and aloofness, as well as a strong sense of chaos on the streets. The distancing of Naples from the rest of Campania has deep roots: when the Romans extended the Appian Way out to the Adriatic, they were careful to stay clear of Greek-dominated Naples, preferring to cross Samnite territory. The bellicose inhabitants of Samnium gradually became integrated into Roman society. Their solid pastoral and warrior values meant that they were less prone to the intricacies and ambiguities of Magna Graecia, generally avoiding the spirals of philosophy. Thus, in the third century BCE, when it was necessary to counter the Carthaginians and King Pyrrhus's war-elephants, the Samnites were useful allies. These ancient Samnite origins and the long-established warrior heritage of the region can still be felt in the populations of the Upper Caserta area, forming the cultural backdrop of the people who have occupied these places for centuries.

It is extraordinary how all these scattered cultural fragments contribute to the formation of the true identity of inland Campania—quite different from the lands under Greek and Etruscan influence, whose refinement and proximity to the sea (in the shadow of Vesuvius) tend

The statue of "Daedalus" by Polish sculptor Igor Mitoraj, at the entrance to the ancient city of Pompeii.
Pages 34–35: Franco Pepe looks out over the Caiazzo region.

to confer a dramatic, theatrical dimension both to the landscape and to public and private life. In contrast we see the sobriety of inland Campania, with its sometimes harsh terrain rising towards the hills, and its distance from the sea. All of this combines with the reserve of its people, tastes, and traditions to create a world that in many respects is still relatively undiscovered.

This is Franco Pepe's territory, and, despite his many trials and successes, it is to this place that he constantly returns, because he truly belongs to this land.

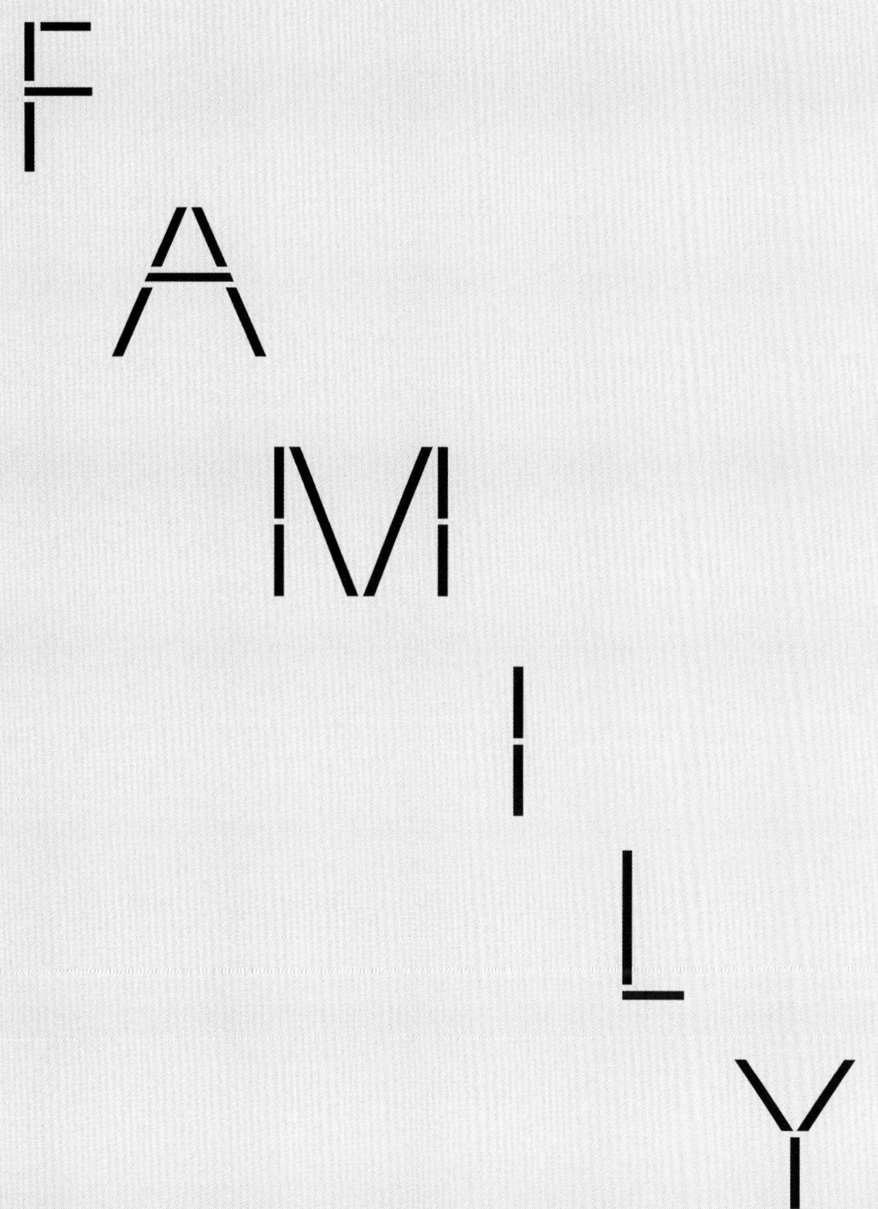

FAMILY

Three Generations

Franco Pepe's story dates back to the early 1900s, providing essential context to his many character traits, including the determination that has propelled him through crucial moments in his life, and his pursuit of goals. The memories stretch back to his grandparents, forming a triptych of three generations of two families who, for almost a century, have been immersed in food: bakers on his father's side, and meat traders on his mother's.

Franco's dad, Stefano, was the eldest of the six children of Francesco (also known as Grandpa Ciccio) and Stefanina, who together owned one of the most popular bakeries in the city. Situated in the Fontanarosa district, its license dated back to 1938. Grandpa Ciccio produced incredible homemade bread in his large wood-fired oven, and the bakery remained active during the Second World War, feeding much of the city's population for over fifty years. The bread was sold in the family shop across the street. Both the bakery and the bread shop were great places for socializing and sharing company—human dimensions that are increasingly lacking today. Shops in small towns were extensions of the public squares, places where people gossiped, resolved disputes, and shared things with one another. When Grandpa Ciccio stopped

(top row from left)
Uncle Nicola, Stefano, Uncle Mario;
(bottom row from left)
Aunt Carolina, Grandma Stefanina,
Aunt Maria, Grandpa Ciccio,
Aunt Antonietta.

Page 36: Franco Pepe's grandfather Francesco—Grandpa Ciccio—at the bread oven; and Franco's dad, Stefano, at the counter.

The rooftops of Caiazzo.

baking bread at the end of each day, people would collect the embers from the oven to put in their "bed warmers" and also to burn in their wood stoves. In the evenings, people used Stefano's oven, with its domed top and still-hot terracotta surface, to cook their own roasts, stews, or even focaccia.

Franco Pepe's grandfather.

In addition to bread, Grandpa Ciccio also sold pan pizza prepared in the morning with the leftover dough from the day before, and on Saturdays he sold pizza by the slice. Customers created makeshift chairs out of the bundles of wood intended to feed the oven, and get-togethers were enjoyed around the hot oven, with a real atmosphere of intimate family-style sharing. Grandpa Ciccio's pizza was very good—so much so that the regular customers were gradually joined by their friends ... and then the friends of their friends. The business grew and expanded, and over the years a small *osteria* was added alongside the bakery—neither a restaurant nor a delicatessen, but one of those unique places that sold only a few types of food designed to be eaten *cum panis*—with bread—its primary product. Grandma Stefanina cooked a wonderful *zuppa di soffritto* (also called *zuppa forte* or *zuppa 'e carnacotta*), an intense soup based on pork offal (lung, trachea, heart, and spleen) with tomato paste, chili pepper, red pepper sauce, bay leaves, and rosemary. In addition to soup, they sold salted sardines, fried cod, some cold cuts and cheeses, and local wine.

Stefano was affectionately known as "the Pole" because of his blond hair and good looks. Extrovert and creative, at a young age he became part of the Caiazzo theater company, and was a well-known *sciupafemmine,* as they say in Campania—a bit of a "ladies' man" or Casanova. He was a gifted soccer player, part of the local team whose iconic nickname was the Vitelloni ("young bucks"). Just like the gang of lads from Romagna described by Federico Fellini in his film of the same name, the Vitelloni strutted along Caiazzo's main street, flirting with the girls and generally having a good time. With his unique charm and blue eyes, it was hard for anyone to resist Stefano. Though he initially studied to be an elementary school teacher, he never finished his training, as his father preferred to have him work at the bakery.

The arrival of Maria, Franco's mother, in Stefano's life marked a decisive turning point. From a wealthy family of traders in livestock and meat, Maria was single-minded and sometimes challenging, but brought with her a toughness and determination, as well as great organizational and management skills inherited from her father

Antonio and her uncle Giuseppe, both skilled traders who over the years had earned the respect of the village.

Prior to Maria and Stefano's marriage, there was no real interaction between the two young people, who had only seen and met each other sporadically over the years. At the time of the marriage, they had barely even kissed. Yet despite this somewhat "arranged" union, Maria and Stefano loved each other right away, and together they built a happy family with three children as well as a solid business. Stefano, the previously "bon-viveur" youth, became an attentive husband, a caring father, and a hard worker with an intuitive flair and meticulous attention to detail. Maria managed the entire family business, drove the car (a fast and very well-kept Opel Cadet), and essentially held the reins of the Pepe family.

In 1961, with the full support of his wife, Stefano opened a pizzeria in Piazza Porta Vetere, right in the center of Caiazzo: the Antica Osteria Pizzeria Pepe. He renovated an old stable, built an oven, and set up seven tables for customers. Compared to the art of bread-making, Stefano found in pizza-making a field of much greater freedom of expression. In addition to the magic of dough, leavening, and cooking, pizza allowed Stefano to come up with creative combinations and pairings of products and flavors, colors, and consistencies.

The pizzeria was a great success with the people of Caiazzo. Open six days a week, it was very demanding, especially as it was Stefano who managed the kitchen, helped only by Giovanni D'Andrea, also known as *Il Fante* ("the soldier"), who grew up learning the trade. In the evening, when the customers arrived, Maria was at the cash register. The oven was always lit, and this was the hub around which everything revolved—even the family.

The front doorway of the
Antica Osteria Pizzeria Pepe.

Stefano arrived at the pizzeria in the morning, brought in the wood and bags of flour, lit the fire, took care of the dough, and also did the cleaning. In the late morning, when the oven was not yet at full heat, he cooked dishes in a pan, since there were usually about ten people who regularly had lunch: baked tagliatelle with peas, eggplant (aubergine) parmigiana, and stewed meat, not to mention a roast chicken that many still remember today.

Grandpa Ciccio with Franco.

(top row from left) Grandma Stefanina, Grandpa Ciccio, Aunt Maria; (bottom row from left) Aunt Antonietta, Franco, Aunt Carolina.

As the eldest of Stefano and Maria's three children, Franco grew up immersed in the daily life of the pizzeria. In addition to his parents, he was looked after by his father's sisters, Maria, Antonietta, and Carolina, and his great-aunt Gerolama, his paternal grandmother's sister. With them he spent a happy childhood, cared for and pampered by family babysitters who loved him like a son.

Franco and his brother Nino attended school in the morning, but in the afternoons they helped at the pizzeria, doing simple jobs like taking dishes to customers.

Neither Stefano nor Maria wanted their children to be pizza chefs. It was considered to be a humble job, and the Pepe family hoped for a less stressful future for their children. Stefano was always wishing for a different life, and there are many who remember his constant refrain: "Study, study, study! Because the job of a *pizzaiolo* is very hard." However, it took a lot of work to pay for their children's schooling, and for this reason the Pepe family spent more time in the pizzeria than within the walls of their home: every day, without holidays, without breaks, without hesitation or doubts.

The 1960s saw an economic boom, which ushered in a cultural shift—the so-called "interesting years"—in which many Italians began to seek a different future for their children. This general sense of wellbeing, and anticipation of what could be achieved with hard work, finally gave the population, even in the poorer south of Italy, hope of an education and social advancement.

Franco trained successfully as a physical education teacher; Nino attended Economics and Business School and became an accountant; and Massimiliano, nine years younger than Franco, studied architecture and carved out, in parallel with his work as a designer, a more administrative and organizational role in the family business.

In 1995 Franco married a local girl, Rita, and began to build a life of his own and dream of a different future. Although he loved his work as a teacher, he was not earning enough to start a family. The support of his clever and sympathetic wife gave him the equilibrium and courage to move forward and get back into the restaurant game. Once again he worked alongside his father, and the rapport between the two became deeper. Franco instinctively understood his father's creativity and came to appreciate his innate inventiveness, sensitivity, and taste. Although Antica Osteria Pizzeria Pepe emerged from deep-rooted traditions, nevertheless the pizzas were made with freshly gathered porcini mushrooms from Matese, fragrant oregano, and other exceptional products. The dough was light, and the pizzas were loved by all in Caiazzo.

When Stefano passed away in 1996, it was as if the earth had opened up under the three brothers. After the funeral, the pizzeria remained closed for two weeks for mourning. When it reopened, it was clear that each of them would have to make the effort to find the time and energy to continue the family business. Franco had become passionate about his father's work, and for him it was an easy decision to give up some of his teaching work, despite the precarious economic situation.

Yet despite numerous attempts, the three could not reach a mutual agreement on how to run things, and family conflicts developed over the ensuing years, leading to some deep divisions. Amid all this strain, Franco understood that the time had come to start a new chapter.

"My father died on May 29, 1996. My son was born two days later—on the actual day of my father's funeral. It was not easy to manage the pain of mourning together with the great emotion of a new life. After two years, my daughter Francesca was born. For me, it was clear from the start that a new strategy and a new future had to begin after our tragic loss. I tried right up to the end not to create family divisions. But the urgency of embracing a different life and my conviction as to the right path we should take—all of this meant that what happened next was inevitable."

Right: Stefano and Maria Pepe.
Below left and right:
A young Franco Pepe.

REVOLUTION

Franco's Way

Two weeks after his father's funeral, when Franco returned to the family pizzeria for the first time, his father's cloth hat and white T-shirt were still lying on the chair. To add to his grief, he realized that there was no actual recipe to allow him to faithfully reproduce his father's pizza.

Up until then, he had only watched the dough being made. For many years, he had handed over the flour and water to go into the wooden *madia* (box) where his father kneaded. He vividly remembered the sight of the coarse salt in his father's hand, and the way he inserted his finger into the water as it dissolved, to check the level of saltiness. But these were only visual fragments, snapshots of memories. There was no recipe, no weight, no quantities.

Franco therefore began to try to physically recreate his father's actions when making the dough. The white plastic bowl that his father used to fill the box became the new unit of measurement, and by reconstructing his father's day step by step, reproducing his specific actions, his various stages of preparation, and the leavening of the pizza, Franco finally created a written record of the measurements and procedures of the original Antica Osteria Pizzeria Pepe recipe.

In the difficult years during which Franco and his brothers shared the task of running the family pizzeria, between 1996 and 2012, Franco embarked on a deep process of self-reflection, wondering whether or not he was a *pizzaiolo,* and thinking about this role in general. Harking back to the words of his father, who had always defined the job as "humble" and "very hard," Franco began to think about how he could improve the nature of the work, and how he could seriously elevate this supposedly "poor" product, which he had inherited first from his grandfather Ciccio, and then from his father Stefano.

Just as he had immersed himself in his studies as a boy, so Franco now set out to "study" pizza, and he began by meeting with the great masters of Neapolitan pizza, since schools and academies specifically dedicated to the subject had not yet come into existence at that time. These were the years during which people were trying in various ways to formalize and recognize Neapolitan pizza, rather than seeking to train a new generation of pizzamakers. Different associations debated and argued about what the "real," "true," or "authentic" Neapolitan pizza was, paying more attention to definitions and specifications than to the current realities of pizza production.

Franco quickly realized that he was not interested in understanding what real Neapolitan pizza was, or what was true or authentic. For him, it was sufficient to appreciate the magic of the dough; the intensity of the flavors to be found in the place where he had grown up; the unique legacy he had received from his family; and the sincere warmth that he received from his customers after they had tasted his pizza. Taking the teachings of his father and grandfather as a starting point, he was able to add to these his own creativity, based partly on a concept of simplicity, partly on the concentration of taste, and partly on the precise recognizability of flavors. By these methods he developed his own very personal and distinctive contemporary pizza.

In the early 1990s, however, the world of pizza was still a long way behind the cutting edge of the world of food, wine, and cuisine. In 1982 *La Gola* appeared: this was the first Italian monthly magazine totally dedicated to "food and material life techniques." In 1986, in the city of Bra, Piedmont, the "Slow Food" movement was founded by Carlo Petrini, visionary and promoter of the idea of "good, clean, fair" culture. In the same year the first gastronomic supplement in Italian journalism was published—*Gambero Rosso* was initially a weekly addition to *Il Manifesto.* Chefs and food promoters, experts, and tasters began to approach food and wine not as if they were closet gluttons but with great pride in the subject, and, above all, a distinct sense of historical awareness and vision. The Michelin and Touring Club guides were joined by new handbooks dedicated to cuisine and restaurants. Within a few years, there was a widespread cultural movement among chefs, wine producers, food artisans, and restaurateurs, pursuing not only the "good" but also the "healthy," preferring the indigenous and the local, exploring innovation and research, and above all focusing on the sheer pleasure of "taste."

Against this backdrop, Franco became increasingly fascinated by the world of cuisine and fine dining, wine, and excellent food artisans. And it was from these perspectives, still somewhat removed from the pizza universe, that he slowly, step by step, reinforced his desire for revolution.

In 2003 Franco found himself catapulted into this new culinary world when Manuela Piancastelli—a journalist with such a passion for wine that she had abandoned her writing career to work as a wine-maker—arrived at Antica Osteria Pizzeria Pepe. Manuela announced to Franco that she and her husband, Peppe Mancini, a lawyer with huge enthusiasm for viticulture, would soon be opening their Terre del Principe winery together with the enologist Luigi Moio.

This was the beginning of a new era for Campania wine, in which native vines were resuscitated, and long-forgotten wines, such as those of the Bourbon era, relaunched. The ancient Pallagrello and Casavecchia wines were among those to be revived.

> "For the grand opening of their winery, they asked me to produce a special pizza. I happily obliged," Franco says, "and I decided to present my father's classic endive calzone. I remembered that my father had always said that this calzone was perfect when paired with a good glass of local wine, so this seemed like the ideal moment to recreate it. During the evening, after the guests had eaten and drunk their fill, I went down into the cellar and was shocked to find there Luigi Veronelli, the absolute prophet of Italian wine, as well as the best food and wine journalists in the country—all of them right next to me, and it seemed impossible that all this was happening a few kilometers from Caiazzo."

After a few months, Luigi Veronelli's magazine *Ex Vinis* published a fantastic article by Piancastelli, highlighting Franco's family pizzeria. This was the first time in Franco Pepe's career that he had featured in a magazine article.

From that moment on, Franco established key links with chefs, producers, and journalists, who would later become dear friends and helpful advisors. This web of relationships allowed him to move beyond the family pizzeria and get to know the wider world of "food." Now he was encountering the chefs, entrepreneurs, and restaurateurs who were beginning to completely change the food sector, focusing relentlessly on quality. It was thanks to this network of contacts that, on Mondays, when the pizzeria was closed, Franco was able to take some of his dough and drive to Rome and Milan.

> "I was curious, and I just wanted to understand haute cuisine, its organization, its recipes, the wisdom to be acquired in the kitchens of great chefs. I watched, and I took notes, always thinking about how to improve my pizza, raise the bar, and draw on my own creativity. It was there that I understood that it was a truly beautiful thing to make things with your own

hands, using your own head and your own ideas."

Knowledge and curiosity were the two fundamental ingredients that allowed Franco Pepe to make this brave leap into a brand-new sector that was only just revealing its potential.

During this phase some new acquaintances were absolutely crucial, such as the chef Antonello Colonna, born and bred in a similar provincial region of Italy, and who, like Franco, had inherited a family business. His success in attracting international visitors to Labico, a small town not far from Rome, was based on his reinvention of classic Roman cuisine, effectively combining his personal traditional approach with contemporary style.

Colonna was one of the first to introduce Franco to the world of haute cuisine. He explained it to Franco, helping him to understand how it worked, and to appreciate the dynamics and balances that regulated an emerging sector finally making itself heard after many years of silence, and creating a team characterized by diverse talents and passions. It was Colonna and his sous chef Marco Martini who invited Franco into their kitchens, giving him unconstrained access to interesting techniques, innovative plating methods, and invaluable experiments. Franco Pepe's pragmatism allowed him to take on board the key elements of these lessons, using them to evolve his own clever ways of transforming ingredients. This enabled him to produce flashes of innovation in his own popular product, introducing a magical simplicity in his concentrations of flavors, as he played with aromatic contrasts.

It was also during this period that Franco first encountered the enthralling flavors of Chef Alfonso Iaccarino. For many years it was said that the world of haute cuisine had found a new center in the village of Sant'Agata sui Due Golfi, where the Iaccarino family had opened their restaurant, Don Alfonso 1890, in 1973, between the Gulf of Sorrento and the Sorrento Peninsula. This was a fine dining restaurant, closely linked to the Campania region, which could virtually spell out the entire history of Italian cuisine with a deceptively simple (yet highly complex!) version of *spaghetti al pomodoro.*

"As a Campanian, it was an honor to have the great master of haute cuisine of my region, Don Alfonso, as my point of reference," Franco points out. "Growing up with such a strong example, able to strip everything back to the basic ingredients, local products, and simplicity, was truly enlightening."

Franco was accompanied on every trip by his young son Stefano—helping, listening, and absorbing everything, just as Franco had done with his own father, but this time in a world with much broader horizons and characterized by an incredible desire for growth.

The world around Franco was slowly changing, and it became increasingly exhausting and isolating for him to return to the family pizzeria and his brothers after these many encounters and rich exchanges. Nino and Massimiliano wanted to continue to manage the family pizzeria as it had been run by their father. In contrast, Franco wanted to be more daring; he wanted to create his own pizzas.

His urge to bring back into the world of pizzerias and pizza chefs something of the world he had come to know outside Caiazzo—the harmonious organization, the precise details, and the desire for haute cuisine—was at first simply a dream. Yet elevating the world of the pizzeria, improving the pizza, assigning real dignity to the role of pizza chef, and putting the local produce and farmers at the center of everything—all these things now became part of Franco Pepe's personal crusade. Strengthened by a new awareness, driven by a courage that many may have seen as reckless and even blinkered, it was clear that the time had come to do something new—something that was his alone, that he could pass on, first and foremost, to his children, preserving the historical essence of the Pepe family. It would be something that could give back real benefits, opportunity, and pride to the region and people of Caiazzo.

This desire for change was not understood by his family, and although Franco wanted to continue working in the family pizzeria in Piazza Porta Vertere, he finally found the courage to upset the apple cart. Amid much conflict, in the winter of 2011 he decided to leave the family pizzeria and open his own business, "a thing that would be just mine alone."

Franco Pepe in his office at Pepe in Grani.

Il Presidente della Repubblica
Ufficiale
Francesco Pepe
Al Maestro
Franco Pepe
Francesco Pepe

A Dream Realized

The past few years had been an important time for Franco, during which he was able to acquire knowledge, know-how, and new techniques—time in which to expand his ideas and simply reflect on things.

The separation from his brothers had begun, and the time had come to take big steps forward on his own, as he planned for his own pizzeria. This would not be a standard pizzeria like those that had been around for decades: places linked to the physical figure of the pizza chef and named after its owner: "Da Franco," "Da Stefano," or "Da Michele," as in much of Italy to date. This would be a new type of pizzeria; an enterprise in which a mixture of "grains" would be blended together to produce something unique: Pepe in Grani.

Franco Pepe's pizzeria had to be a forward-looking place, capable of restoring dignity to the pizza chef; a place where new generations could be trained, and in which the knowledge of the past could be intertwined with clear-thinking about the future. This would be a "slow restaurant" pizzeria based around real partnerships with small local producers. It had to be a "training center for skilled artisans," where pizza could be made with 1930s-style dough, enhanced by a contemporary edge. It needed to revolve around the oven and pizza, in a constant dialogue with the kitchen, producing recipes with tried and tested flavors, just like those in the *osteria* of Grandpa Ciccio and Grandma Stefanina.

In 2011, Franco embarked on a new and ambitious phase of planning, in which ideas were rapidly thrown around, urgently needing to be formalized into a place, a style, a name, and a language that could clearly express and summarize the project's current state of play. What was really needed was a physical "box" in which to place all these new ideas, so the search for a property in the city became the main priority.

"I drove around Caiazzo every day looking for a space that could contain my ideas. It needed to be a bright space with a good view over the surrounding area, but it also needed to have a strong connection with the city's past. One day I found a building that had been uninhabited for thirty years. It was in terrible condition, but it just had an incredible energy. I closed my eyes and imagined the movement of the waiters, the smell of the wood and the oven, and I understood that this was the right place for my dream," says Franco, still emotional at the memory today.

Having found the location—the steep, narrow alleyway of the Vicolo San Giovanni Battista—it was time to consider the physical form of the building. This was the beginning of Franco's collaboration with the architect Beniamino Di Fusco. With sensitivity and style, Di Fusco transformed this abstract project into a design, then a prospectus, and then an actual construction site. The final process was characterized by careful restoration and delicate revitalization, combined with sheer inventiveness, creativity, and an embracing of the future. The property, occupying several floors, was a stately building, which, according to the white stone coat of arms surmounting the arched entranceway, dated back to 1788. Wherever possible, the features of the original building were restored as meticulously as if this were an archaeological excavation, but wherever it was necessary to create new volumes and dimensions, the ancient stone was combined with newer materials such as iron and weathered steel.

During the restoration work, a tiny ancient oven without a flue was discovered—this had most likely been used to dry "hosts" (unleavened bread used to symbolize Christ's body in the Eucharist). Although the original building was not a chapel, it had certainly been inhabited by priests, and the presence of the oven was likely proof of this. This discovery also gave the project an unexpected mystical—and highly auspicious—aspect.

In the spring of 2012, Luigi Cremona, an assiduous journalist and editor of the *Italian Touring Club* guide, arrived at the Antica Osteria Pizzeria Pepe, where Franco was still working:

"It was lunchtime when I entered the pizzeria overlooking the square at the entrance to the historic center. I ate two very good items, a pizza margherita cooked to perfection and a calzone made with curly endive, which had none of the usual heaviness you'd expect; it was surprisingly light, and when you opened it the room filled with the scents of the garden.
I understood that I had in front of me not just any pizza chef but a true master. My compliments had an immediate effect on Franco, and he approached me at the end of the meal, saying: 'Come with me and I'll show you my secret dream.' We crossed the piazza into the alleyways of the historic center, mostly abandoned

at this time, heading down a humble, hidden-away street. Halfway down, there was a ruined building and the mayhem of a construction site. We entered, and Franco showed me the corner where the pizza oven was being built brick by brick. This was not all: it wasn't just a room with an oven in it. There were actually two more floors, and on top of them a roof-terrace. Up there, as we reveled in the panoramic view that opened up, Franco told me the details of his dream. I wrote the next day: the first luxury pizzeria in the world is being created—and I wasn't wrong."

Since Franco's budget was limited, the process of construction was very quick (taking only six months), with many friends and skilled workers contributing voluntary labor. Even his son Stefano regularly came by before and after school to lend a hand. Franco organized everything as if he were coaching a sports team, drawing on his past as a physical education teacher and athlete. The six months of construction were divided up into a precise schedule, similar to the organization of a mountain-bike race or an obstacle course. The finishing line—when all construction had to be completed—was crossed on schedule, with the entire team gathered together. Many of the workers who contributed to the creation of Pepe in Grani stayed on to work for the company, and, after months of careful training, some even became expert pizza chefs.

It was clear from the start that the new project would be no normal pizzeria. One room on the first floor was dedicated to the production of the dough. The spaces within the kitchen and oven were calculated precisely to accommodate the culinary activity. The exterior, equipped with a veranda, was designed to allow diners to commune with the terraces and walls of the city, with its hidden citrus groves and aromatic herbs. An ancient staircase provided access to the roof-terrace overlooking the valley, and at sunset the view was transformed by the rosy colors of the evening light.

Now Franco's dream needed a name that was somehow meaningful and fun at the same time; one that clearly communicated its essence. Thanks to Francesco Palladino, a brilliant young communications and internet specialist from Caserta, the perfect name was created by playing around with the word *pepe* (pepper), the original meaning of Franco's surname, and the word *grani* (grains), referring directly to the most vital ingredient: the cereals used for the pizza base. Finally, the new brand contained the central preposition "in," which had the effect of creating a sense of motion, evolution, and the idea of progression, but also described the effort required to gradually assemble a "thing" made up of many pieces; a new, different, unique entity comprising innovation and evolution.

On October 14, 2012, Franco Pepe's new project, Pepe in Grani ("peppercorns") was officially launched.

GARGIULO

DOUGH

Hands, Ingredients & Ovens

The magic of a pizza is in its dough, which is the hallmark of a *pizzaiolo* and the identity of a pizzeria. A host of variables make a dough special and unique, and Franco Pepe has never shared these out of respect for his history and the legacy he received from his father, Stefano.

Anyone can mix flour with yeast, water, and salt. Some will end up making an awful pizza; others will manage something mediocre; while some will succeed in making a magnificent pizza. The quality of a dough is not so much determined by the flour, water temperature, or the

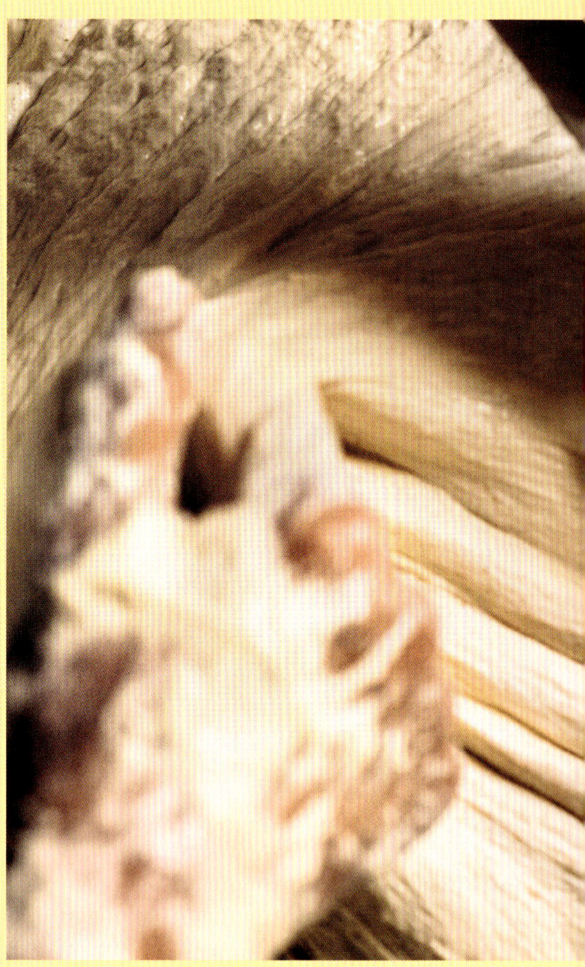

ambient temperature; nor does it depend solely on the type of yeast, its freshness, or how it is stored; or on the way the water is incorporated into the dough; whether the dough is made by hand or kneaded in a mixer; the way it is leavened; the ingredients and equipment used; or the type of oven and baking temperature. What makes the real difference is the touch, sensitivity, and energy of the human, the individual—their desire to make a simple dough into something extraordinary.

"I was fortunate to grow up with the daily experience of my father's pizzeria. I inherited the profession very gradually, by seeing and observing my father work. It was only when I felt deep down that pizza had great value in my life, when I decided to open Pepe in Grani, and that pizza really represented me, my family, and my land—only then—that my dough changed. It was only by working with the many professionals with whom I have collaborated over the years, only through the experiences that made me grow, that my dough was able to grow, rise, and evolve. This is a necessary premise, because it makes no sense for me to simply provide a recipe, a set of measures. Otherwise, it's

pointless to explain the steps, timing, and leavening method required to make a proper dough. A successful dough greatly depends on how you embrace the work, how you interpret the ingredients, and how you understand your surroundings."

Dough is the most difficult thing about pizza; it is the most delicate step and the most fragile balance in the whole process. Although many believe it to be impossible and outdated, Franco Pepe's dough is still strictly made by hand even today.

Natural flours, water, salt, yeast, and *criscito*—a little of the levain left over from the previous day—are the ingredients that, day after day, go into the *madia,* the wooden box where they are gradually mixed together using both arms and hands. The time it takes to make the dough varies greatly, depending on the ingredients, as well as the temperature, relative humidity, and time of day.

"Dad would wake up in the morning and make the dough, and he would bake the pizza in the evening," Franco explains. "Each dough reflects the type of work you have to do, how big the pizzeria is, and how many staff you have. Today," he says, "I think I've achieved an ideal

balance in my dough. I calibrated everything to the millimeter, looking back to my past and respecting my father's recipe, but I've reproduced it on an exponential scale, thanks to the way my staff is trained, and technology."

Each pizza has a cycle that takes about thirty hours. Kneading begins in the afternoon, and the pizza is served on the evening of the following day. Today only Franco and a small group of *pizzaioli,* coordinated by Stefano, handle the dough and satisfy the growing demand for Pepe in Grani's pizza.

There is a room in the pizzeria dedicated to the dough and laid out around the old wooden *madia,* which is where the magic begins. When you watch Franco Pepe at work, you can see how. He senses something intangible, at times incomprehensible, that tells him that this formless mass, for many imperfect and unfinished, has now reached its *punto di pasta* or "dough point"—its peak development. His professional experience and the use of all his senses show him the precise moment to stop kneading, when to let the dough rest, and when to gather the dough into a ball for proofing, after which it will be rolled out, toppings added, and baked.

It is a tactile, visual, and olfactory experience that allows him to recognize the condition of the dough at a glance, by feel, and possibly a sniff.

There are no kneading machines in Franco's laboratory, but temperature and humidity are meticulously managed. Technology is essential to monitor the dough and to achieve the very fragile balance that relies on minimizing the amount of yeast used, extending the hours of rising, and careful control of temperature. Heat drives the dough and cold keeps it in check; this part is easy to understand. However, which flours to use, when to change the temperature, and when and by how much to reduce the amount of yeast is known only to the *pizzaiolo.*

The processes followed at Pepe in Grani are born out of respect for a tradition handed down over three generations, and in the deep conviction that the past can be key to an innovation whose very strength is its ancient, archaic, rural, and preindustrial elements.

Even today, only handmade wooden *madie* are used for kneading the 600–700 pizzas it produces daily in winter and 900–1,000 in summer, just as it only uses handcrafted wooden *tavote,* rectangular wooden boxes for proofing the dough balls. Plastic is not used due to the danger that microplastic residue may be incorporated into the dough, and also because plastic containers do not allow the dough to breathe; it is an inert material that does not interact with living matter, unlike naturally porous wood, which allows air and moisture to be exchanged.

Flour

One of the most important collaborations over the years, which has come to represent the evolution of Pepe in Grani's dough, is with the Piantoni family, who operate Molino Piantoni, a flour mill in the province of Brescia. Franco Pepe has been buying their flour for more than eleven years. And not just any flour—theirs is an exclusive blend made from mostly Italian grains, which is determined by Franco Pepe and Fausto Valbusa from one day to another according to the year, the season, the temperature, and the quantities of dough to be produced. Different grains sourced from different regions are milled a few weeks before use and subsequently combined to create a product capable of being turned into light, tasty, and easily digested pizzas.

Although the composition may differ from month to month, the flour is made to a standard formula that varies with the seasons. In each of its versions, it has enough protein to ensure a good stretch but not too much elasticity; because the dough must be able to stretch without retracting, elasticity is not important. The lowest protein content is 13 percent, the minimum needed to allow the crust to develop its aroma.

Franco shares the Piantoni family's values, as well as a strong friendship and mutual esteem. Indeed, their collaboration is so close that it also includes the use of batches of experimental flours at different times of the year, which produce a particularly fragrant dough with special aromatic notes.

Today's process echoes the past, when Papa Stefano would also make doughs using different flours, taking scoops of flour from different sacks resting on the floor near the marble kneading slab where he worked and combining them to make a dough.

> "Mixing flours is a crucial operation that Molino Piantoni enabled me to carry out with lots of experimentation and technology," Franco Pepe explains. "A great deal of trial and error led to the creation of '0 Pepe,' a blend of three flours that change according to the season and harvest year, which allows me to produce dough of a very high standard that is constantly evolving."

0 Pepe is produced exclusively for Franco Pepe and is not on the market.

0 Pepe flour—Franco's custom flour blend created in collaboration with Molino Piantoni.

Cooking

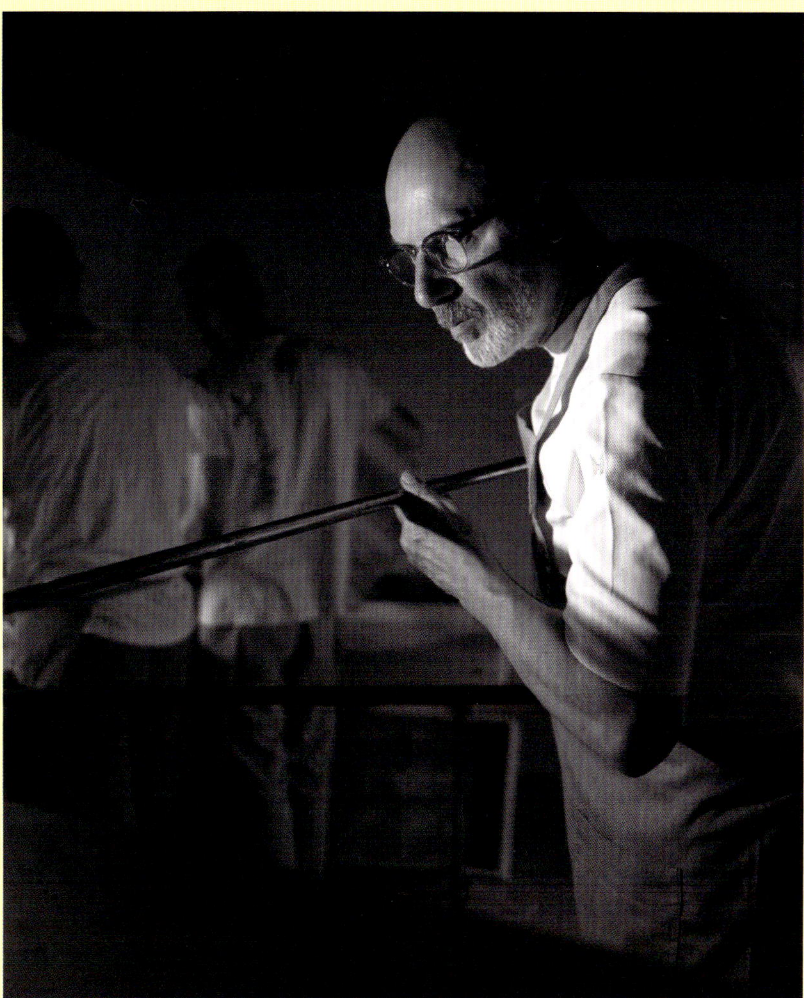

Pepe in Grani pizzas are either baked in a wood-fired oven or deep-fried.

When deep-frying, only high-linoleic sunflower oil is used at a temperature never exceeding 430°F / 220°C. Changing the oil daily and careful monitoring with a special electronic testing device that detects not only the temperature but also residual substances and the level of oxidation in the oil means that deep-frying is not only a delicious cooking option but also a healthy one.

When it comes to baking in a wood-fired oven, it is important to remember that not all ovens are suitable for baking pizzas. The ovens at Pepe in Grani are traditional Neapolitan domed ovens lined with 2.5-inch / 60-mm refractory brick and a cooking floor made of Sorrento biscuit, a type of terracotta made from clay rich in volcanic silica and pumice, which is particularly porous and capable of heating quickly and retaining heat for a long period. Pepe in Grani only uses certified dried beechwood, which produces a fairly high temperature and does not create a lot of embers, which is ideal for making a clean and smooth pizza.

All ovens are different, depending on their location, materials, age, and flue length. The most important thing is to know your oven well and to understand how the temperatures inside it vary. This allows you to rotate the pizza and move it backward and forward to the points with the desired temperature. In the zone closest to the burning wood, the oven floor temperature reaches 840°F / 450°C. In the zone farthest from the fire, on the side opposite the burning wood, the temperature range is 750–790°F / 400–420°C, whereas the temperature does not exceed 700°F / 370°C at the oven mouth.

Classic pizzas, such as Margherita and Marinara, are cooked in about 1 minute 30 seconds, 2 minutes at most, at a temperature alternating between 790°F / 420°C and 840°F / 450°C. A Calzone, on the other hand, is cooked more slowly, in about 2 minutes 30 seconds. At first, a Calzone should be introduced at 790–840°F / 420–450°C to allow it to puff up. After about 20 seconds, it should be brought closer to the oven mouth to keep it from burning. There, the second cooking stage takes place at a temperature of 700°F / 370°C for another 2 minutes 30 seconds.

Regardless of the oven you use, pizza is always cooked with the oven mouth open. It is essential to be able to watch and quickly turn the pizza as it cooks. Because the temperature is not even throughout the oven chamber, it is up to the *pizzaiolo* to move it to the hottest part of the oven or to the oven mouth to achieve a properly cooked and unburnt pizza.

"I teach kids how to bake pizza and how to work out the oven temperature just as my father taught me for years. To be a *pizzaiolo,* you have to understand the different colors the bricks turn with temperature and to interpret the sounds the floor makes when touched by the metal of the peel. While it's essential to use your senses, I also explain to my kids today how useful and important technology is. A good laser thermometer can help and make your work faster, but it will never be enough. First comes human know-how, followed by checking with technology," says Franco.

Secret Recipe

As you may have guessed by now, the recipe for Franco Pepe's pizza is an illusion: it depends on too many seasonal, environmental, ingredient, and human variables. Franco has repeatedly told me that some things deserve to be kept secret. "It's a way to show respect for the people who have passed on their knowledge to me," he insists. "Not everything can be explained and described the way they are in cookbooks."

Throughout the writing of this book, I tried to take note of what to do and what not to do, and to memorize procedures and techniques in an attempt to offer readers a basic blueprint that they can use to make their own pizza at home, despite Franco trying to dissuade me several times. The result is my simple recipe for an excellent homemade pizza (it should make enough for six to eight individual pizzas or two pan pizzas). Of course, it is nothing like a pizza made in Caiazzo, but that will be clear to you by now.

Italian type 0 flour .... **2 lb 3oz / 1 kg**
Water .... **23¾ fl oz / 700 ml**
Fine salt .... **1 oz / 30 g**
Fresh brewer's yeast .... **1½ tsp / 4 g**

Pizza Dough, Day 1

In a container, preferably a small *madia* or wooden bowl, put 1 lb 12 oz / 800 g of the flour on one side and 23 fl oz / 680 ml of water at 50°F / 10°C on the other side.
Add the salt to the water and dissolve.
Combine the flour with the water and start to knead, folding the dough over on itself. Once the flour is incorporated, dissolve the yeast in ¾ fl oz / 20 ml water at 77–82°F / 25–28°C and add to the dough.
Continue to knead, adding another 3½ oz / 100 g of the flour.
The dough will still be quite runny. At this point, rest the dough for 30 minutes at room temperature (75–79°F / 24–26°C).
After 30 minutes, the dough should have stabilized. Using a dough scraper, gather the dough together in the container. Then turn the dough out onto a floured wooden work surface and knead by folding, sprinkling with the remaining flour as needed, until you have a soft, smooth dough.
Transfer the dough from the work surface to a glass bowl and cover with plastic wrap (cling film).
Let the dough rest for 3 hours at room temperature, then refrigerate overnight at 39–43°F / 4–6°C.

Pizza Dough, Day 2

The next morning, take the dough out of the refrigerator and keep it at room temperature for at least 2 hours. Place the dough on the work surface, then divide it into 7-oz / 200-g portions. Gather each portion into a ball, using a repeated dough-rounding motion with the hand, with the dough still on the work surface—a technique known as "pirling." Place the balls in a wooden proofing box dusted with flour until they come to a temperature of about 70°F / 21°C. The dough will be ready to make into pizzas after around 90 minutes.

On a floured marble work surface, gently press and stretch the balls into disks, leaving the edges all around unpressed to form the crust. Add toppings as desired (see recipes to follow), and bake in a pizza oven at 840°F / 450°C for 2–4 minutes, depending on the oven.

If using a static oven at home, it's better to make two pan pizzas. Oil your hands and spread the dough (you may need around 1 lb 2 oz–1 lb 5 oz / 500–600 g per pizza) directly into an oiled pan and let rest for 30 minutes. Bake at 430°F / 220°C for 20–35 minutes, depending on the thickness of the pizza and topping.

A Note on Toppings

The toppings of every Pepe in Grani pizza contain ingredients, preparations, and products that are often rare and unattainable, the unique result of a strong network of important ties that Franco Pepe has built up over the years with producers. The resulting friendships have also led to mutual collaborations that have served to improve those products and the pizzas served at Pepe in Grani.

"Growing together" is a motto for Franco Pepe, and by exchanging information and working with others to beat new paths, he has placed his own stamp on his work. Franco has never considered for a moment that he has reached his ultimate goal or achieved perfection, either for a pizza or a particular product. Instead, "evolution" is the most appropriate term he uses to describe the way his ideas are constantly being reworked as they become intertwined with insights, advice from producer friends, and memories of recipes from home.

Each ingredient and product is from the countryside around Caiazzo—from the Matese mountains to the coast—sourced from both the highlands and the valleys of the Volturno river and its tributaries. They are the tiles of a gastronomic mosaic that Franco Pepe creates in his pizzas to tell the story of his land.

Some products are one of a kind and impossible to substitute. Their specific names tell the story and reveal the characteristics of the product, as well as outline the work of incredible people: the fragrant and intense oregano grown in the Matese mountains, the sweetest tomato varieties from Campania, Caiazzane olives and their extra virgin olive oil, buffalo mozzarella and *fior di latte* (cow's milk mozzarella), buffalo ricotta, Conciato Romano cheese, Crisommola del Vesuvio apricots, Cetara anchovies, and Alife onions.

RECIPES

This book contains thirty recipes that serve as milestones in the story of Franco Pepe's work. More than recipes, they are culinary representations of the stages in his life and career—unexpected encounters, surprises, and discoveries that are associated with particular events, anecdotes, and recollections—and each one comes with an introduction that explains a little of its background.

Pizza a Libretto

Antica Osteria Pizzeria Pepe would close for lunch every day except Wednesdays, when the open-air market took over the main square of Caiazzo. For the occasion, the family's historic metal food warmer, known as a *stufa*, would be filled with numerous small pizzas that were folded into triangles and sold wrapped in paper, not sizzling from the oven but lukewarm.

Giovanni D'Andrea, nicknamed *Il Fante* ("the soldier"), was Stefano Pepe's right-hand man at the pizzeria. This skilled baker and handyman would be tasked with filling the food warmer and walking around the market several times until all the pizzas were sold.

Even today at Pepe in Grani, it is still possible to order this Pizza a Libretto (or Pizza a Portafoglio—"wallet pizza"), which tells us so much about the history of the Pepe family and of pizza itself. This iconic form of street food, typically hawked in the alleyways of Naples, would often be made with dough left over from the previous day, and made the pizzeria and pizza even more popular as food for the masses. "Anybody can walk into my pizzeria today and taste my dough for two euros fifty. For me, this still has important, very important, social value," Franco points out.

Ingredients for one pizza

Pizza dough → PAGE 75 .... **5 oz / 150 g**

San Marzano dell'Agro Sarnese-Nocerino PDO tomato sauce .... **2 3/4 oz / 80 g**

Chopped Polesano PDO white garlic .... **1 tsp / 2 g**

Extra virgin olive oil .... **1 1/2 tsp**

plus extra for seasoning

Matese oregano, dried .... **pinch**

Pizza a Libretto

Stretch the dough into a disk with minimal crust, then top with the tomato sauce, garlic, and oil, and bake for 1 minute 30 seconds at 790–840°F / 420–450°C.

Remove from the oven, season with oregano and oil, and fold in half.

Let rest in a food warmer until ready to serve.

Endive Calzone

This calzone was created by Franco's father, Stefano. Its simplicity says a great deal about the innovative spirit of this *pizzaiolo* from the 1960s, who was both traditional and purist on the one hand, and inherently revolutionary and forward-looking on the other. The calzone is filled with raw curly endive (frisée), rather than sautéed and highly seasoned endive as tradition would have it. The anchovies, capers, olives, and extra virgin olive oil are also added raw.

Unlike the Neapolitan tradition, which involves pricking the calzone to allow the steam to escape, this calzone is delicately "stuffed" and then sealed to create a proper steam chamber, like a pressure cooker, which is capable of tenderizing the vegetable as it cooks.

In the Pepe family tradition, the dough is slightly thinner, the cooking time is shorter, and the calzone is very light.

In the mouth, the endive is sweet and soft, while retaining a firm texture; all the flavors are easily distinguished, and there is a perfect balance between the filling and crisp crust.

An olive farmer at work at the Azienda Sangiovanni, a family-run farm not far from Caiazzo. For three generations the estate has proudly cultivated the rare Caiazzana olive, a variety that grows on ancient, large trees throughout the area.

Ingredients for one calzone

Pizza dough → PAGE 75 . . . . **10 oz / 280 g**
Salt-packed Ischia capers . . . . **2 tsp / 4 g**
Curly endive (frisée) . . . . **3½ oz / 100 g**
Cetara anchovy fillets in oil . . . . **1 oz / 30 g**
Caiazzane black olives, pitted. . . . . **⅓ oz / 10 g**
Extra virgin olive oil . . . . **2 tsp**
plus extra for drizzling

Endive Calzone

Rinse all the salt from the capers and soak in water for at least 2 hours, or ideally 24 hours.

Stretch the dough into a disk without creating a crust.

After washing and thoroughly drying the endive (frisée), cut into pieces and place in the center of the dough disk. Add the anchovies, capers, and olives and drizzle over the 2 teaspoons of oil.

Fold the top half of the disk over the filling to create a half-moon. Press the edges well to seal, and trim the excess dough with a knife or plain pastry cutter.

Drizzle the surface of the calzone with more oil and bake for 20 seconds at 790–840°F / 420–450°C, then move to the oven mouth for 2 minutes 30 seconds at 700°F / 370°C. Once the calzone is cooked, drizzle with more extra virgin olive oil and serve.

Pinsa Conciata del '500

Pizza Mastunicola is believed by many people to be the first pizza in history, although there are two versions of this story. Some believe pizza Mastunicola to have been named after its inventor, Mastro Nicola, a baker whose oven was located in the Rua Catalana in Naples, not far from the Castel Nuovo, in the years before the arrival of tomato and mozzarella; it was topped with *nzogna* (pork fat), pepper, pecorino cheese, and basil.

For others, the name of the original pizza is derived from the Neapolitan word for basil, *vasuinicola*, since a lot of it went into the topping of pizza Mastunicola.

"Without going into a historical discourse that would serve no purpose, I wanted to call this pizza "*pinsa*" to echo the original history of pizza without tomato and mozzarella," Franco Pepe explains.

Liliana Lombardi from Le Campestre prepares the Conciato Romano cheese. Together with her husband Francesco, son Manuel, and daughter-in-law Eulalia, they continue the traditional method of making this ancient cheese, which is aged in terracotta amphorae.

le campestre

Francesco Lombardi stirs the curd that will be ladled to create Conciato Romano cheese at Le Campestre.

"In 2011, at an event at Don Alfonso restaurant, together with Manuel Lombardi and Elisia Menduni, I decided to pay tribute to the historic Mastunicola recipe and make it special, imagining what pizza was like before Columbus.

"Alfonso Iaccarino, with a cigar in his mouth and a satisfied expression, arrived in the forecourt in front of the bakery with a small *apette* (three-wheel van) loaded with crates of fruits and vegetables from his magnificent garden at Punta Campanella.

Francesco Lombardi presses fresh sheep curd into molds while making Conciata Romano at Le Campestre.

Conciato Romano cheese ages in its outdoor cheese cage at Le Campestre.

"I had just baked a pizza bianca with lardo di nero Casertano, and Manuel was flaking Conciato Romano cheese over it as I was sprinkling it with fresh basil. Elisia could not resist and suggested that I add fresh figs. She tore them into pieces by hand and spread them over, adding a final drizzle of oil. The whole thing worked instantly. Since then, whether fresh or as jam, I have been adding the sweetness of figs to the traditional Mastunicola recipe. Besides, they give the pizza the sweetness that the tomato probably would have given the old *pinsa* in the 1500s!"

Liliana and Francesco Lombardi.

ZA
834 FC
le campestre

Ingredients for one pizza

Pizza dough → PAGE 75 **........................ 10 oz / 280 g**
Black Casertano pig lardo .... 1 tsp / 5 g
Extra virgin olive oil .... 1½ tsp
Cilento fig jam .... 2¾ oz / 80 g
Conciato Romano cheese, medium-aged, grated ....
.. ½ oz / 15 g
Fresh basil leaves 4–5
Matese oregano, dried .... pinch
Black pepper .... to taste

Pinsa Conciata del '500

Stretch the dough into a disk, leaving a uniform crust around the entire circumference.

Starting in the center, cover the surface with the lardo, making sure to leave an even layer of pork fat. Drizzle the entire pizza with oil, then season with plenty of pepper and bake the pizza for 1 minute 30 seconds at 790–840°F / 420–450°C.

Once cooked, cut the pizza into 6 slices and add a teaspoon of fig jam, or fresh fig wedges if in season, to each slice and top with the grated Conciato Romano cheese. The secret of this pizza is achieving the right balance between the intensity of the cheese and the sweetness of the jam, so take care not to add too much cheese. Finish by adding basil leaves and sprinkling with oregano. Season with more pepper if desired.

Il Sole nel Piatto

This pizza was created in 2012, when the Pepe brothers took part in a documentary produced by Roberto Gambacorta for Rio Film, and directed by Alfonso Postiglione, *Il Sole nel Piatto* ("The Sun on a Plate"), whose title is borrowed from the Neapolitan poet Salvatore di Giacomo.

As Franco explains, "This pizza is a map of a region's geography. A land that revolves around a volcano that is thousands of years old and that brings forth unique produce from the mountains to the sea: Cetara anchovies, Mozzarella di Bufala di Campania cheese, Piennolo del Vesuvio cherry tomatoes, Caiazzane black olives, and fragrant oregano from the Matese Mountains."

Harvesting the olives in the orchards of the Azienda Sangiovanni estate.

Ingredients for one pizza

Pizza dough → PAGE 75 .... 10 oz / 280 g
Mozzarella di Bufala di Campania PDO, sliced .... $4\frac{1}{4}$ oz / 120 g
Piennolo del Vesuvio PDO canned cherry tomatoes, drained .... $3\frac{1}{2}$ oz / 100 g
Caiazzane black olives, pitted .... $\frac{3}{4}$ oz / 20 g
Extra virgin olive oil .... $1\frac{1}{2}$ tsp plus extra for drizzling
Cetara anchovy fillets in oil .... $1\frac{1}{2}$ oz / 40 g
Fresh basil leaves 8
Matese oregano, dried .... pinch

Il Sole nel Piatto

Stretch the dough into a disk, leaving a uniform crust around the entire circumference.
Top the pizza with sliced mozzarella and the tomatoes. These cherry tomatoes are canned in a light brine and retain the flavor of fresh tomatoes. Add the olives, drizzle with the $1\frac{1}{2}$ teaspoons of oil, and bake for 1 minute 30 seconds–2 minutes at 790–840°F / 420–450°C. Once cooked, add the anchovies, basil, and oregano to the pizza, drizzle with extra virgin olive oil, and serve.

Porkaserta

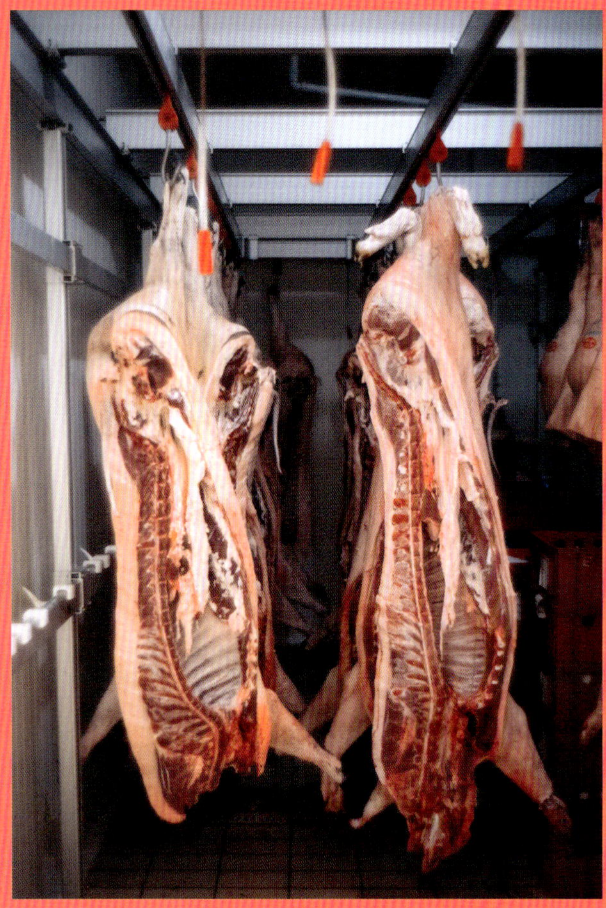

Maialino nero Casertano (Black Casertano pigs), ready to be made into sausage and other products.

"I wanted to pay tribute to one of the emblematic products of the province of Caserta, the Black Casertano pig, so this strongly flavored pizza tells of its interesting intensity. It features an explosion of the acorn and chestnut flavor given by the marbled meat and fat of Black Casertano pigs, which are raised in a semi-wild state in my area."

Images of these small slate-gray pigs—a relative of the Cinta Senese, Nero Siciliano, and Noir of Bigorre breeds—can be found in the ancient frescoes of Capua, Pompeii, and Herculaneum. Even then, people enjoyed the taste of its easy-melting fat and its forest aromas.

Sausage made from *Maialino nero Casertano* (Black Casertano pigs) is hung to dry.

Ingredients for one pizza

Pizza dough → PAGE 75 **........................ 10 oz / 280 g**
San Marzano dell'Agro Sarnese-Nocerino PDO canned tomatoes in sauce .... 3½ oz / 100 g
Fine salt .... ⅓ tsp / 2 g
Fior di latte (cow's milk mozzarella), drained and sliced .... 2¾ oz / 80 g
Smoked Caciocavallo Silano PDO cheese, sliced .... 1½ oz / 40 g
Casertano dry-cured pork sausage flavored with wild fennel, thinly sliced .... 2 oz / 60 g
Extra virgin olive oil .... 1½ tsp
Matese oregano, dried .... pinch

Porkaserta

Crush the canned tomatoes by hand, and season with the salt.
Stretch the dough into a disk, leaving a uniform crust around the entire circumference.
Add the crushed tomatoes to the center and spread over the pizza, avoiding the crust. Then top with slices of the fior di latte cheese, the Caciocavallo Silano cheese, and thin slices of sausage.
Drizzle with the oil and bake for 1 minute 30 seconds–2 minutes at 790–840°F / 420–450°C.
Once cooked, sprinkle the pizza with oregano and serve.

La Ritrovata

Luigi Filippo Ammendola, a great Vesuvian farmer, holding Piennolo tomatoes.

La Ritrovata ("Rediscovery") pizza was Franco Pepe's attempt to recreate and rediscover the taste and smell of his father Stefano's pizza marinara, the pleasure of which was in its simplicity and clean flavors resulting from the balance of topping ingredients. Very few changes were made to the original, but the quest to give La Ritrovata absolute balance was the key to a revolutionary evolution.

The pizza, dedicated to Franco's father, is not topped with just any tomato, but with two emblematic tomatoes with different flavors and textures. In addition to the Matese oregano, Franco includes basil for crunch. The anchovies are added only after baking to keep them tender and juicy. The flavor of garlic is evenly distributed through the use of garlic-infused oil. The olives and capers are dried and used with meticulous care so that their flavor does not overpower.

The addition of anchovies makes this pizza a reflection of the Mediterranean, giving it a perfect balance of fiber, protein, and omega-3 fatty acids. "The evolution is in the detail, in enhancing what my father, Stefano, was doing unconsciously, following his sense of *buono e giusto*, doing things the right way, which it's up to me to uphold today."

Boxes of San Marzano tomatoes.

Ingredients for one pizza

Pizza dough → PAGE 75 .... **10 oz / 280**
Garlic .... **1 clov**
Salt-packed capers .... **1 ts**
Caiazzane black olives, pitted. ....
San Marzano dell'Agro Sarnese-Nocerino PDO tomat
sauce .... **1¾ oz / 50**
Piennolo del Vesuvio PDO canned tomato halves. ....
.... **3½ oz / 100**
Extra virgin olive oil .... **1 tbs**
plus extra for drizzling
Fresh basil leaves **5–**
Cetara anchovy fillets in oil .... **1¾ oz / 50**
Matese oregano, dried .... **pinc**
Sunflower oil, for frying

La Ritrovata

Peel, degerm, and mince the garlic.

To tone down the intense flavor of the capers and olives, we prefer to dry them and then grind the olives into a powder. Rinse, drain, and spread the capers out on a baking sheet. Place the pitted olives on a separate baking sheet. Dry both in the oven at 140–160°F / 60–70°C for 2–3 hours. Let cool, then grind the olives into a powder using a mortar and pestle or spice grinder.

Stretch the dough into a disk, leaving a uniform crust around the entire circumference. Top with the tomato sauce and add the tomato halves and minced garlic. Drizzle the pizza with the tablespoon of olive oil and bake for 1 minute 30 seconds–2 minutes at 790–840°F / 420–450°C.

Fry the basil leaves in sunflower oil for a few seconds.

Once cooked, arrange a few capers and anchovies on top of the pizza, sprinkle evenly with the black olive powder and oregano, add the basil leaves, and finish with a drizzle of olive oil.

Margherita Sbagliata

"This pizza symbolizes the founding of Pepe in Grani; it represents the inner creativeness that I had been trying to express for years."

Pizza Margherita Sbagliata ("Pizza Margherita Gone Wrong") marked the beginning of a new chapter. In fact, the use of that adjective "wrong" in the name itself was so liberating that nobody could fail to notice that something different was happening, a new course had been taken. For the first time, with a provocation never before seen, it was as if Neapolitan tradition had become outdated and the basic rules of its identity no longer mattered.

"If my pizza doesn't meet traditional standards, I don't care! I'll call it 'wrong,' but at least it will be MY pizza!" Franco stresses.

Franco Pepe's Margherita Sbagliata came about for a very simple, technical reason: the riccio tomato could not withstand the heat of the oven. Subjecting it to that heat changed its original flavor and did not enhance its qualities. So Franco decided to add it after baking the pizza, twisting and overturning the original idea of the traditional pizza Margherita, for which cooking the tomato is an essential part. This change to the timing of the addition of the topping ingredient, and the sharp differentiation of individual flavors on the pizza was an important and crucial step in Franco's journey.

Riccio tomatoes sit in the back of the car of Domenico Barbiero, owner of La Sbecciatrice, supplier of Pepe in Grani.

The Pizza Margherita Sbagliata that was created in 2012 in Vicolo San Giovanni Battista, Caiazzo, is a pizza Margherita whose ingredients are exalted to the maximum, whose flavors are respected in a way that is both healthy and functional, and whose playfulness and design emerge effortlessly and without fear of judgment by others.

Eight red stripes on a white background in vivid dialogue with bright green drops of basil sauce—as an art critic might say—is a pizza that is finally freed from convention and ready to be considered a true work of art. "We must remember that we Italians are also from the country of art and design. Why shouldn't a pizza also play with these dimensions, illustrating shapes, geometries, and color combinations, as well as balance of flavors and taste? That can also be called evolution!" Franco vehemently concludes.

Opposite and below: Riccio tomatoes, used in Margherita Sbagliata, are harvested and stored at La Sbecciatrice.

Ingredients for one pizza

Pizza dough → PAGE 75 .... **10 oz / 280 g**
Riccio tomato sauce .... **4 1/4 oz / 120 g**
Fine salt .... **pinch**
Fresh basil sauce → BELOW .... **1/3 oz / 10 g**
Mozzarella di Bufala di Campania PDO, sliced ....
.... **5 oz / 150 g**
Extra virgin olive oil .... **1 1/2 tsp**

Ingredients for the fresh basil sauce

Fresh basil leaves .... **1 3/4 oz / 50 g**
Extra virgin olive oil .... **2 tsp**

Margherita Sbagliata

Pour the tomato sauce into a strainer over a bowl and let it drip through the mesh until very thick and creamy. Transfer the sauce to a squeezy bottle, season with a pinch of salt, and chill to 39°F / 4°C in the refrigerator.
For the basil sauce, blanch the basil leaves in boiling water for a few seconds. Drain and immediately shock in a container of water with plenty of ice. This will preserve their intense green color. When cool, drain the leaves well and blend, adding the extra virgin olive oil and a few ice cubes. When a smooth liquid forms, transfer to a squeezy bottle and refrigerate at 39–41°F / 4–5°C.
Stretch the dough into a disk, leaving a uniform crust around the entire circumference.
Arrange the mozzarella slices on the pizza, drizzle with the extra virgin olive oil and bake for 1 minute 30 seconds–2 minutes at 790–840°F / 420–450°C.
Once cooked, finish the pizza by piping eight small strips of tomato sauce over the cheese and drizzling over dots of basil sauce.

La Scarpetta

Vincenzo Aufiero, producer of the San Marzano tomatoes (right) used at Pepe in Grani, in his hand-watered tomato, vegetable, and herb garden.

This pizza came about after a lunch one August in Montegrosso, a town not far from Andria, in the heart of Puglia. There, over 30 years ago, the forward-thinking chef Pietro Zito decided to open his traditional restaurant Antichi Sapori ("Flavors of Old"). The restaurant showcased the Zito family's recipes, local traditions, and particularly the produce grown in their own garden.

"Pietro's story struck a chord in me," Franco says. "It felt very familiar and similar to my own. It strengthened in me a compelling sense of belonging, of my ties to family and tradition that I had been reflecting on for years. That day I had an incredible tomato pasta, with different textures created by the use of different tomatoes; it was an uncooked sauce whose temperatures and intensity made for an outstanding flavor explosion.

"This pizza was created from the memory of my *scarpetta*, using a piece of bread to soak up the last tomato left on the plate from that incredibly delicious pasta."

Ingredients for one pizza

Pizza dough → PAGE 75 .... 10 oz / 280 g
Cream cheese → BELOW .... 4¼ oz / 120 g
Fresh Ciliegno tomatoes .... 3½ oz / 100 g
Dried San Marzano PDO tomatoes .... 3½ oz / 100 g
Tomato sauce .... 2 oz / 60 g
Fresh basil leaves 5
Garlic .... 1 clove
Fior di latte (cow's milk mozzarella) .... 1¾oz / 50 g
24-month-aged Parmigiano Reggiano or Grana Padano cheese, shaved .... 2 oz / 60 g
Freeze-dried basil pesto powder .... ½ tsp / 2 g

Ingredients for the cream cheese

Whipping cream .... 10 fl oz / 300 ml
12-month-aged Parmigiano Reggiano or Grana Padano cheese, grated .... 5 oz / 150 g

La Scarpetta

To make the cream cheese, put the whipping cream into a saucepan and bring to a boil. Remove from the heat, add the grated cheese, and blend with a stick blender until creamy and smooth.

Wash the fresh tomatoes, then place in a blender with the dried San Marzano tomatoes, tomato sauce, fresh basil, and garlic clove and blend to a smooth cream. If too liquid, leave it to strain through a fine-mesh sieve.

Stretch the dough into a disk, leaving a uniform crust around the entire circumference. Spread the shaped pizza evenly with 4¼ oz/120 g cream cheese (the remainder will keep in the refrigerator for 2–3 days), top with the fior di latte cheese, and bake for 1 minute 30 seconds–2 minutes at 790–840°F / 420–450°C.

Once cooked, cut the pizza into 6 slices, and in the center of each slice place 1 level tablespoon of the creamed tomato (the remainder will keep in the refrigerator for 2 days), then add a sliver of Parmigiano Reggiano or Grana Padano, and sprinkle with freeze-dried basil pesto powder.

Ciro

Kiton is an amazing fashion company with roots in the Campania region since 1968 and an extraordinary model of entrepreneurship and quality. Its founder, Ciro Paone, who sadly passed away a few years ago at the age of 88, was a close friend and mentor to Franco. The company's focus on luxury, absolute quality, style, and the highest standards of craftsmanship made it a role model for Pepe in Grani.

"When I went to visit him in Arzano, not far from Naples, I was enchanted by the many tailors who were making one-of-a-kind jackets and other garments with such dedication. All by hand. From then on, Ciro Paone's motto, 'The best of the best plus one,' stuck in my head for a long time and often helped me think about the details, about that small leap forward that makes it possible to achieve excellence by paying attention to the little things," Franco explains.

"In 2017 Ciro Paone invited me to an event at Pitti Uomo, and it naturally came to me that I should 'tailor' a new pizza around him. I created the Cono Ciro, which started out as a kind of stuffed *seada sarda*, before turning into a calzone that was cut and vertically mounted to form a small, delicious, beautiful, and elegant cone."

Ingredients for two small cones

Pizza dough → PAGE 75 . . . . **3½ oz / 100 g**
Caiazzane black olives, pitted . . . .
Cream cheese → PAGE 122 . . . . **1¾ oz / 50 g**
Arugula (rocket) pesto → BELOW . . . . **1 oz / 30 g**
Sunflower oil, for deep-frying

Ingredients for the arugula (rocket) pesto

Arugula (rocket) . . . . **3½ oz / 100 g**
Extra virgin olive oil . . . . **3 tsp**
Pine nuts . . . . **½ oz / 15 g**
Fine salt

Ciro

Dry and grind the olives following the instructions on page 112 to create a black olive powder.
For the pesto, blanch the arugula (rocket) leaves in lightly salted boiling water for a few seconds. Drain and immediately shock in a large bowl of ice water. Drain and transfer to a blender with the oil and pine nuts and blend.
Stretch the dough into a disk.
Spread the cream cheese in the center of the pizza and add 1 oz/30 g of arugula pesto (the remainder will keep in the refrigerator for 2–3 days).
Fold the top half of the disk over the filling to create a small half-moon.
Press well on the edges to seal and trim off the excess dough.
Heat plenty of sunflower oil in a large pan to 410–430°F / 210–220°C, and deep-fry the calzone for about 90 seconds, until golden. Cut in half and stand the halves upright to prevent the filling from spilling out.
Sprinkle over the olive powder.

Memento

"We must never forget where we come from and what makes our land so special. That's why I wanted to call this pizza Memento: so I never forget where my roots are," says Franco Pepe.

This garden vegetable pizza is a tribute to the Caiazzo region and to healthy eating. It is vegan—containing only wheat, legumes, and vegetables—showing that pizza can also be completely plant-based. Instead of cheese, chickpea cream adds mellowness, while raw chicory adds a bitter, pungent, and grassy contrast to the palate.

Onion restores sweetness and balance, as well as adding crunch in fried form.

The onion field of Antonietta Melillo,
producer of the Alife onion.

Ingredients for one pizza

Pizza dough → PAGE 75 .... **10 oz / 280 g**
Extra virgin olive oil .... **2 tsp**
plus extra for dressing
Alife onion, julienned .... **⅓ oz / 10 g**
Alife onion purée → PAGE 133 .... **5 oz / 150 g**
Caiatini chickpea cream → PAGE 133 .... **2 oz / 60 g**
Wild chicory .... **1½ oz / 40 g**
Black pepper .... **to tast**

Memento

Heat the 2 teaspoons of oil in a pan to 355°F / 180°C. Pat the julienned onion strips dry with paper towel, and fry in the oil for 2 minutes.

On the work surface, stretch the dough into a disk, leaving a uniform crust around the entire circumference.

Spread the pizza with the onion purée and bake for 1 minute 30 seconds–2 minutes at 790–840°F / 420–450°C.

Once cooked, slice the pizza and top each slice with chickpea cream followed by wild chicory dressed with oil, the crunchy fried onions, and seasoned with pepper.

Ingredients for the Alife onion purée

Extra virgin olive oil .... 2 3/4 fl oz / 80 ml
Alife onions, peeled and minced .... 14 oz / 400 g
Fine salt .... 1 tsp / 5 g

Ingredients for the Caiatini chickpea cream

Dried Caiatini chickpeas.................. 10 oz / 300 g
Bay leaf 1
Garlic .... 2 cloves
Fine salt .... to taste
Extra virgin olive oil .... 3 tsp

Alife Onion Purée

To make the onion purée, heat the oil in a large saucepan and add the onions. Sauté the onions until soft and until all the liquid they release has evaporated. Then add a glass of water (about 6 fl oz / 180 ml) and let cook over low heat. Once the water has evaporated and the onion is cooked, remove from the heat and purée with a stick blender. Season with the salt and leave to cool before using on the pizza. The remainder will keep in the refrigerator for 2–3 days.

Caiatini Chickpea Cream

For the chickpea cream, soak the chickpeas in water overnight. On the day of cooking, fill a saucepan with water, add the bay leaf and garlic, and salt the water. Then add the soaked chickpeas and cook for 2 hours. Drain the chickpeas, removing the bay leaf and garlic, and blend in a blender, gradually adding the oil. The remainder will keep in the refrigerator for 2–3 days.

Bufala Profumata

The combination of buffalo meat with the quintessential product made from its milk creates an intense and fragrant pizza.

Only pepper and garlic oil are added to the pizza before baking. Thickly sliced mozzarella is added after just under a minute to heat through without melting and altering its texture. Then a drizzle of lime is added to the mozzarella for a sour contrast to its creaminess. After baking, the pizza is topped with thin slices of buffalo bresaola, oven-toasted sesame seeds, and lime zest. This is a summer pizza with different textures and fresh citrus notes.

Ingredients for one pizza

Pizza dough → PAGE 75 .... **10 oz / 280 g**
Garlic oil, for drizzling → BELOW
Black pepper .... **to taste**
Mozzarella di Bufala di Campania PDO, sliced ....
.... **7 oz / 200 g**
Buffalo bresaola .... **2¾ oz / 80 g**
Lime juice .... **1 tsp**
Sesame seeds, toasted .... **1 tsp / 3 g**
Lime zest, grated .... **1 tsp / 2 g**
Extra virgin olive oil .... **1 tbsp**

Ingredients for the garlic oil

Garlic .... **1 clove**
Extra virgin olive oil .... **10 fl oz / 300 ml**

Bufala Profumata

For the garlic oil, wash the garlic clove and press to a pulp. Add the garlic pulp to the oil in a bowl and leave to infuse for 6 hours.
Stretch the dough into a disk, leaving a uniform crust around the entire circumference.
Drizzle with garlic oil, season with freshly ground black pepper, and bake for 1 minute 30 seconds at 790–840°F / 420–450°C.
Halfway through cooking, add the sliced mozzarella and return the pizza to the oven.
Once cooked, top the pizza with slices of buffalo bresaola, lime juice, sesame seeds, lime zest, and the extra virgin olive oil.

Sensazione di Costiera

"Between the dough and the toppings, I wanted to bring fragrance, lightness, and flavor to pizza fritta with this pizza," says Franco Pepe. "My aim was to completely overturn the canon governing deep-fried pizza by creating one that was light and fresh, one that evokes the sea and its smells through the freshness of citrus fruits."

Caiazzo is only 12½ miles (20 kilometers) from Caserta and 31 miles (50 kilometers) from the sea. Although standing on a hill a mere 660 feet (200 meters) above sea level, Caiazzo almost seems a mountain town.

When Franco was a child, the sea was like a mirage. His mother would occasionally take the children to the Lido Delizia beach resort in Scauri on the bus. On some Mondays, when the pizzeria was closed, his father Stefano would also leave for Scauri in his straw yellow Fiat 127, but only ever for the day. "Unfortunately, in my life," Franco explains, "I never had the opportunity to go on vacation with my parents that involved a night in a hotel, or a period of a few days. For us, because of work, the most vacation we could have was a trip to Scauri from morning until night."

To dream of the sea, sometimes all you need is a Sensazione di Costiera ("Feeling of the Coast") pizza at 660 feet (200 meters) above sea level: the flavor of parsley that reminds you of fish, the zest of Sorrento lemons, and Cetara anchovies, along with a slice of vine tomato, perhaps from Punta Campanella, on a deep-fried pizza.

Boats sit in the Bay of Naples.

Ingredients for one pizza

Pizza dough → PAGE 75	**7 oz / 200 g**
Garlic powder	**1 tsp / 3 g**
Vine tomatoes, thinly sliced	**2 3/4 oz / 80 g**
Chili powder	**3/4 tsp / 2 g**
Cetara anchovy fillets in oil	**2 oz / 60 g**
Fresh parsley, chopped	**1/3 oz / 10 g**
Lemon zest, grated	**2 tsp / 4 g**
Sunflower oil, for deep-frying	

Sensazione di Costiera

Stretch the dough into a disk and prick it all over with a fork.
Heat plenty of sunflower oil in a large pan to 410–430°F / 210–220°C, and deep-fry the pizza for about 90 seconds. When the pizza is golden brown, remove from the oil, dry on paper towels, and cut into 6 slices.
Sprinkle the pizza with garlic powder and arrange the tomato slices in the center of each slice. Sprinkle the center of each tomato slice with a pinch of chili powder and top with anchovy fillets.
Sprinkle with chopped parsley and finally grate a little lemon zest over each slice.

Ananascosta

"One day in Hong Kong, a journalist asked me if I had ever thought of putting a Hawaiian pizza on the menu. As a matter of fact, it had never occurred to me. I seized on the opportunity to reflect more broadly on topping ingredients, such as fruit, that were absolutely 'not classic' in terms of tradition, and began to think of a pizza that might overcome these prejudices."

Hawaiian pizza—which is pizza with pineapple—is believed to have been invented by a Greek-Canadian pizza maker in the 1960s. It has since diverged into a large number of variations around the world. According to the most popular recipe, the topping contains cooked ham and pieces of canned pineapple spread over mozzarella cheese. Franco eliminated the cooked ham, replacing it with a lightly salted cured ham, *prosciutto crudo dolce*, and introduced chilled fresh pineapple, so that in addition to flavor, this pizza was also enhanced by contrasting temperatures and textures. The name Ananascosta—a play on the words *ananas*, "pineapple", and *nascosta*, "hidden"—comes from the pineapple being hidden, wrapped inside a roll of ham, and inserted into the cone-shaped deep-fried pizza. This "surprise" is meant to challenge the very widespread prejudice that fruit should never go on pizza. The result is thrilling: the freshness of the cold pineapple, in combination with the deep-fried calzone case, is an explosion on the palate, helped by the fattiness and delicious flavor of the *prosciutto*.

Ingredients for two small cones

Pizza dough → PAGE 75 .... **3½ oz / 100 g**
Grana Padano cream cheese → PAGE 122 .... **¾ oz / 20 g**
Licorice powder .... **scant ½ tsp / 2 g**
Fresh pineapple, chilled .... **¾ oz / 20 g**
Prosciutto crudo dolce, thinly sliced ....**1 oz / 30 g**
Sunflower oil, for deep-frying

Ananascosta

Stretch the dough into a disk and spread the cream cheese in the center. Fold over the top half of the disk and seal the dough to form a small half-moon. Trim off the excess dough.

Heat plenty of sunflower oil in a large pan to 390–430°F / 200–220°C, and deep-fry the pizza for about 90 seconds, until golden.

Once cooked, cut in half and stand the halves upright. Sprinkle a pinch of licorice powder inside the cones.

Wrap the chilled pineapple inside a slice of prosciutto and insert into each cone, then sprinkle with more licorice powder and serve.

Pastiera Fritta

This pizza is a dessert made of pizza dough that came into existence through the creativity of Stefano Pepe (junior) as a tribute to a great Campanian pastry chef, Alfonso Pepe.

Stefano had met him when he was about 16 years old, following his father to an event in New York City. When all the event participants met at Capodichino Airport before their departure, the master pastry chef immediately asked Stefano to help carry hundreds of small rum babas that he did not want to travel in the cargo hold. Stefano willingly obliged, and a beautiful understanding soon formed.

The event in the Big Apple was a great success, and when it came to an end, Alfonso offered all the guests *graffe fritte*, doughnut-like clouds of deep-fried dough. Stefano had seen him work and fell in love with pastry making.

When the master pastry chef passed away following an illness in 2020, Stefano decided to dedicate this fried dessert to him. According to Stefano, "This light cloud honors a great master and ambassador of our land."

Ingredients for two small cones

Pizza dough → PAGE 75 .... **3½ oz / 100 g**
Pastry cream → PAGE 149 .... **2 oz / 60 g**
Fior di latte (cow's milk mozzarella) .... **¾ oz / 20 g**
Superfine (caster) sugar .... **⅓ oz / 10 g**
Ground cinnamon .... **1 tsp / 5 g**
Roasted hazelnuts .... **¾ oz / 20 g**
Candied fruit (pumpkin, citron, orange, amarena cherry) .... **¾ oz / 20 g**
Orange zest, grated .... **1 tsp / 2 g**
Sunflower oil, for deep-frying

Pastiera Fritta

Stretch the dough into a disk and spread 2 oz / 60 g of the pastry cream and fior di latte cheese over the center. Fold over the top half of the disk and seal the dough to form a half-moon. Trim off the excess dough. Heat plenty of sunflower oil in a large pan to 390–430°F / 200–220°C, and deep-fry the pizza for about 90 seconds, until golden.
Once cooked, pat dry with paper towels and sprinkle with sugar and cinnamon. Cut in half and stand the halves upright, then add the toasted hazelnuts, candied fruit, and a sprinkling of orange zest.

Ingredients for the pastry cream

Egg yolk	1½ oz / 40 g
Superfine (caster) sugar	¾ oz / 25 g
Italian type 00 flour, sifted	1 oz / 35 g
Fresh milk	6¾ fl oz / 200 ml
Vanilla bean (pod)	1

Pastry Cream

For the pastry cream, mix the yolks with the sugar in a bowl, incorporate the sifted flour, and set the mixture aside.

Bring a little water to a boil in a tall pan for use as a bain-marie for cooking the pastry cream.

Heat the milk with the seeds of the vanilla bean (pod), then place everything together in a heatproof bowl set over the bain-marie and mix with a whisk to prevent lumps from forming. When smooth, let the pastry cream cool. Keep in the refrigerator and use within 1 day.

Straccetti with Honey & Rosemary

Opposite and above: Bee smoker and hives at Azienda Sangiovanni.

This is a simple dessert devised for the use of scraps left over from making pizza. The dough is cut into strips, known as *straccetti* ("rags"), and deep-fried. The strips are then topped with fragrant honey produced in the Caiazzo area, creamy ricotta cheese, and fresh rosemary. This delicious dessert brings back memories of childhood snacks.

Ingredients for one portion (serves two)

Pizza dough → PAGE 75 . . . . 3½ oz / 100 g
Superfine (caster) sugar . . . . ½ oz / 15 g
Ground cinnamon . . . . 1 tsp / 5 g
Fresh rosemary, chopped . . . . 1 tsp / 3 g
Orange zest, grated . . . . to taste
Caiazzo wildflower honey . . . . 1½ oz / 40 g
Vanilla bean (pod) . . . .
Buffalo ricotta cheese . . . . 1¾ oz / 50 g
Sunflower oil, for deep-frying

Straccetti with Honey & Rosemary

Roll out the dough evenly on a work surface and use a pastry cutter to cut out a large number of strips, ½ inch (1 cm) wide and 2 inches (5 cm) long.
Heat plenty of sunflower oil in a large pan to 390–430°F / 200–220°C, and deep-fry the strips for about 60 seconds, until golden.
Mix two-thirds of the superfine (caster) sugar with the cinnamon and use it to dust the fried strips.
Arrange the straccetti on a plate and sprinkle with chopped rosemary, grated orange zest, and honey. Combine the vanilla seeds from the pod (bean) with the remaining sugar, stir through the ricotta cheese, and serve in a small bowl alongside the straccetti.

Crisommola del Vesuvio

"Over ten years ago, I learned from customers in the Vesuvius area that many local apricot growers preferred not to pick fruit rather than sell it for less than its worth. The price of apricots from northern Italy was so competitive that it was better to let the crop rot on the trees. I definitely wanted to try those rare and endangered Crisommole del Vesuvio apricots. After tasting them, I swore I would do something to revive this amazing product. That's how this pizza was born," says Franco Pepe. Thanks to the precious work of the Perna and Ammendola families, today the Crisommola del Vesuvio is experiencing a new lease of life. For having triggered demand and breathed new life into this special apricot, Franco Pepe was recognized as an "Honorary Citizen" of Somma Vesuviana in 2020.

Crisommole del Vesuvio apricots growing on the hills of Mount Vesuvius.

F.lli SANNINO
F.lli SANNINO
F.lli SANNINO

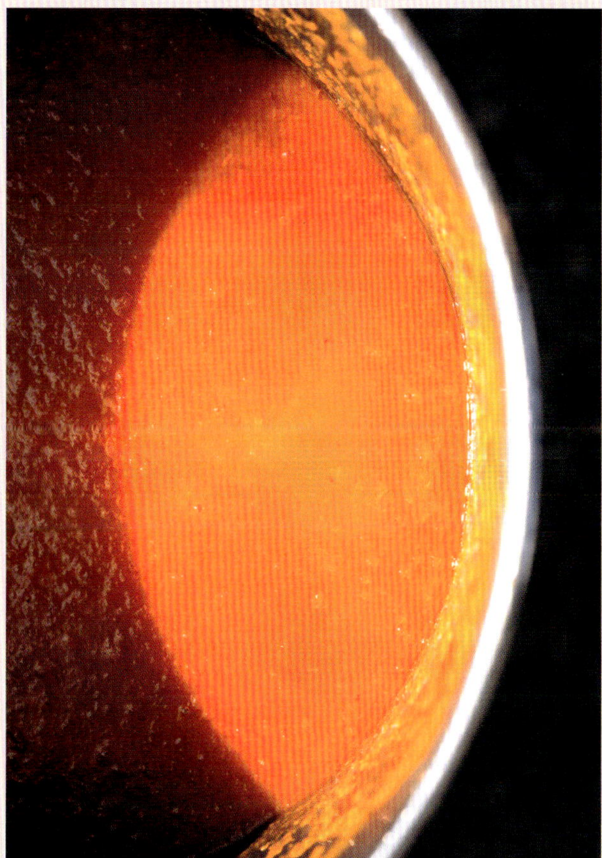

Above and pages 156–157: Freshly picked apricots are sorted and prepared for jam-making by Annamaria Rosaria Aliperta and Pierfrancesco Ammendola; Opposite: An apricot farmer takes a break from harvesting.

Ingredients for one pizza

Pizza dough → PAGE 75 .... **7 oz / 200 g**
Caiazzane black olives, pitted **3**
Buffalo ricotta cheese .... **2½ oz / 70 g**
Lemon zest, grated .... **generous 2 tsp / 5 g**
Hazelnuts, coarsely chopped .... **1 oz / 30 g**
Crisommola del Vesuvio apricot jam .... **2¾ oz / 80 g**
Small fresh mint leaves ....
Sunflower oil, for deep-frying

Crisommola del Vesuvio

Dry and grind the olives following the instructions on page 112 to create a black olive powder.
Put the ricotta into a deep mixing bowl, add the grated lemon zest, and whisk gently to a smooth and silky consistency. Set aside.
Lightly toast the hazelnuts in a nonstick skillet (frying pan) to an amber color. Let cool on a cold surface.
Stretch the dough into a disk.
Heat plenty of sunflower oil in a large pan to 410–430°F / 210–220°C, and deep-fry the pizza for about 90 seconds. When the pizza is golden brown, remove from the oil, dry on paper towels, and cut into 4 slices.
Using a pastry (piping) bag, pipe over the top with the lemon-flavored ricotta and apricot jam. Sprinkle with the chopped hazelnuts and olive powder. Add a mint leaf to each slice before serving.

L'Alifana

"This pizza is a special tribute to a delicate and fragrant product that I am proud to have helped revive and develop," says Franco Pepe. "My intention was to thank Antonietta Melillo and her strength with a pizza that is as intense as she is!"

L'Alifana is an expression of the land south of the Matese mountains, centered on the town of Alife: not only the sweetness and delicacy of the ancient Alife onion, rediscovered and reintroduced, but also the smoke of the cellars where cured meats are refined, the scents of earth and wood of the ancient stone quarries, and the intensity of Matese oregano.

Antonietta Melillo left her job in 2011 to dedicate her tim to cultivating the local Alife onion, which was on the verg of extinction.
Pages 164–165: Alife onions hang in frames on the farm.

Opposite: Antonietta Melillo, with trays of her onions (above).

Ingredients for one pizza

Pizza dough → **PAGE 75**	**10 oz / 280 g**
Fior di latte (cow's milk mozzarella)	**3 1/2 oz / 100 g**
Pancetta, thinly sliced	**2 3/4 oz / 80 g**
Alife onions, julienned	**2 3/4 oz / 80 g**
Smoked scamorza cheese, sliced	**2 oz / 60 g**
Extra virgin olive oil	**1 1/2 tsp**
Matese oregano, dried	**1 tsp / 2 g**

L'Alifana

Stretch the dough into a disk, leaving a uniform crust around the entire circumference.

Add the sliced fior di latte cheese, thinly sliced pancetta, onions, and scamorza cheese. Drizzle with the oil and bake for 1 minute 30 seconds–2 minutes at 790–840°F / 420–450°C.

Once cooked, finish the pizza with a generous sprinkling of Matese oregano.

Profumi del Matese

The Matese mountain range is an imposing massif that forms the boundary between the regions of Molise and Campania. Over the centuries, it has been a refuge for brigands, monks, partisans, and anarchists. Today, thanks in part to these centuries of isolation, it is a small natural paradise, an unspoiled habitat for nature and wildlife.

Here, among peaks and plateaus, lakes, caves, and pristine forests, herds of buffalo and cattle are reared and allowed to graze. It is a land of field crops, but also of orchards and mushroom-filled woodland. Profumi del Matese ("Scents of the Matese") is a pizza inspired by the fragrance and flavors of this land.

Sunset over the Matese mountains.

Ingredients for one pizza

Pizza dough → PAGE 75 .... **10 oz / 280 g**
Fior di latte (cow's milk mozzarella) ...... **3½ oz / 100 g**
Pecorino del Matese cheese .... **1¾ oz / 50 g**
Extra virgin olive oil .... **1½ tsp**
Cherry tomato confit in extra virgin olive oil .... **1½ oz / 40 g**
Matese oregano, dried .... **1 tsp / 2 g**

Ingredients for the sautéed porcini mushrooms

Matese porcini mushrooms .... **3½ oz / 100 g**
Extra virgin olive oil .... **1 tbsp**
Black pepper

Profumi del Matese

For the sautéed porcini mushrooms, clean the mushrooms by brushing and wiping with a slightly damp cloth, then slice. Heat the oil in a skillet (frying pan), add the mushroom slices, and season with pepper. Let cook on low heat for 10–15 minutes.
Stretch the dough into a disk, leaving a uniform crust around the entire circumference.
Tear the fior di latte cheese into pieces by hand, then top the pizza with the fior di latte cheese pieces, small cubes of Pecorino, and sautéed mushroom slices. Drizzle with olive oil and bake for 1 minute 30 seconds–2 minutes at 790–840°F / 420–450°C.
Once cooked, add the cherry tomato confit and sprinkle with the oregano.

Montanara

Made from very few, very simple ingredients, this small tomato-smeared and deep-fried pizza is the quintessential dish that has fed Neapolitans for centuries. It actually has deep roots in the popular cooking of the mountain regions of Campania, to which the name *montanara* ("of the mountains") attests, despite becoming an icon of Neapolitan street food over the course of centuries.

It is typically made using leftover pizza dough from the day before, fried to order and, at best, topped with tomato sauce, a sprinkling of grated cheese, and a basil leaf. Originally, these kinds of snacks, known as *marenna*, which fed the poorest inhabitants of Naples, did not normally come with a topping.

In the movie *The Gold of Naples* (1954) by Vittorio De Sica, the deep-fried pizzas made by the magnificent Sophia Loren were "plain" and "on credit," evidenced by a sign in the movie that stated "Eat today and pay in eight days."

Opposite: Sunset in Naples.
Below: Mount Vesuvius looms over the Neapolitan Peninsula.

Ingredients for one pizza

Pizza dough → PAGE 75 . . . . **7 oz / 200 g**
Polesano PDO white garlic, chopped . . . . **1 clov**
Extra virgin olive oil . . . . **2 tsp**
San Marzano dell'Agro Sarnese-Nocerino PDO tomat
sauce . . . . **2 3/4 oz / 80 g**
Fine salt . . . . **to tast**
Matese oregano, dried . . . . **generous 1 tsp / 3 g**
plus extra for topping
Fresh basil leaves **4**
Sunflower oil, for deep-frying

Montanara

Sauté the garlic in the olive oil and add the tomato sauce.
Season with salt and plenty of dried oregano and let simmer until the sauce is rich and thick.
Stretch the dough into a disk and prick all over with a fork.
Heat plenty of sunflower oil in a large pan to 410–430°F / 210–220°C, and deep-fry the pizza for about 90 seconds. When the pizza is golden brown, remove from the oil, dry on paper towels, and cut into 6 slices.
Top with the hot tomato sauce and add a little more dried oregano and the fresh basil leaves.

Pizza in Teglia is prepared in pans using the previous day's dough, and is designed to serve four people.

Pizza in Teglia

Of all the pizzas featured in this book, this is the only pan pizza and, to date, is not yet on the menu at Pepe in Grani. It is made for staff, events, and by special order only. This pizza is made with leftover dough from the day before, and Stefano Pepe, Franco's father, used to make it every morning. It is topped with hand-torn pieces of tomato, sprinkled with oil and oregano, and baked for 7–8 minutes when the oven is not yet at full temperature. The crust is also thick and fluffy. This concept is very different to pizza baked on a pccl and needs greater recognition. It is easy to reheat and is also delicious cold.

Ingredients for one round pan pizza (serves four)

Pizza dough → PAGE 75 **.................... 1 lb 2 oz / 500 g**
Extra virgin olive oil .... 4 tsp
plus extra for greasing
San Marzano dell'Agro Sarnese-Nocerino PDO tomato sauce .... 7 oz / 200 g
Piennolo del Vesuvio PDO canned tomato halves .... 3½ oz / 100 g
Garlic, chopped ....1 clove
Matese oregano, dried .... generous 2 tsp / 5 g
Fresh basil leaves ....

Pizza in Teglia

Grease a round baking tray (¾-inch / 2-cm deep, with a diameter of 13 inches / 33 cm) with oil. Stretch the dough out on the greased baking tray.

Rest the dough for about 1 hour, depending on the temperature. Ideally, it will need to rise by at least half its volume. Press on the dough randomly with your fingers to create depressions.

Top the dough with the tomato sauce and Piennolo tomatoes, 4 teaspoons of oil, and the chopped garlic, and bake at 535°F / 280°C for 7–8 minutes in a wood-burning oven, without adding wood to produce a live flame and with the oven door closed.

Sprinkle with oregano and fresh basil before serving.

Grana Pepe e Fantasia

Throughout history, *quattro formaggi* ("four-cheese") pizza has been made with cheese left over from making the day's pizzas. Grana Pepe e Fantasia, on the other hand, is intended to be a special, purpose-made *quattro formaggi* pizza containing four cheeses with four different textures that celebrates high-quality cheeses and their varied flavors. A cream made with a hard cheese, such as Grana Padano or Parmigiano Reggiano, and small pieces of caciocavallo cheese are spread all over the surface of the dough disk for the first baking stage. Then, before cooking completely, the pizza is taken out of the oven and egg yolk is added. Pecorino Romano cheese is then grated over the crust and the pizza returned to the oven to bake for another 10–20 seconds. Finally, once cooked, a sprinkling of cheese chips adds crunch and texture.

This pizza revisits many different flavors, such as those of carbonara and breakfast eggs and bacon. It is also a clever way of using up scraps, such as cheese rinds.

Ingredients for one pizza

Pizza dough → PAGE 75 .... **10 oz / 280 g**
Crispy smoked bacon .... **2 oz / 60 g**
Cream cheese → PAGE 122 .... **3½ oz / 100 g**
Smoked caciocavallo cheese .... **1½ oz / 40 g**
Pecorino Romano PDO cheese, grated ..... **1½ oz / 40 g**
Extra virgin olive oil .... **1½ tsp**
Pasteurized egg yolk .... **1 oz / 30 g**
Cheese chips → PAGE 185 .... **1 oz / 30 g**
Zest of 1 lime, grated
Black pepper

Ingredients for the cheese chips

Rind of Grana Padano or Parmigiano Reggiano .... **3½ oz / 100 g**

Grana Pepe e Fantasia

To prepare the crispy bacon, cut the bacon into ⅕-inch / 5-mm cubes. Heat a nonstick skillet (frying pan) for a few minutes and then dry-fry the bacon cubes, gradually removing the fat as it is released, until well toasted and crispy. Drain off all the remaining fat and pat the crispy bacon dry with paper towels.

Stretch the dough into a disk, leaving a uniform crust around the entire circumference.

Spread with the cream cheese, add thin strips of caciocavallo cheese, drizzle with oil, and bake for 2 minutes at 790–840°F / 420–450°C. Take the pizza out of the oven and sprinkle the crust with grated Pecorino Romano cheese. Use a squeezy bottle to pipe a spiral of egg yolk over the pizza, except for the crust.

Finish baking for 40–50 seconds. Once cooked, add the crispy bacon, cheese chips, grated lime zest, and season with pepper.

Cheese Chips

For the cheese chips, shave off the waxy coating from the hard cheese rinds. Thinly slice the rinds and spread them over a plate.
Cook for 20 seconds in a microwave oven, then let cool and break them into small crispy flakes.

Pitta Fabula

This pizza is inspired by Greek and Middle Eastern pita sandwiches, and many southern Italian *pitta* (pie and pastry) dishes, such as the famous Calabrian delicacies *pitta chicculiata*, a pie filled with tuna, anchovies, tomatoes, olives, and capers; *pitta mpigliata*, a pastry stuffed with honey, walnuts, and dried fruit; and *pitta nchiusa*, a pastry made with almonds, pine nuts, walnuts, raisins, cinnamon, and white wine. An interesting version, *pitilla*, is also made in Puglia. There the dough is kneaded with olives or raisins, baked in a wood-fired oven, and the resulting bread stuffed with ricotta cheese, tomatoes, onions, or fried bell peppers.

This pizza is folded to create a pocket and filled with such special ingredients as cured ham, creamy and captivating Fabula cheese (buffalo milk cheese with a bloomy rind), and fig jam. A savory and sweet, crunchy and creamy combination, refreshed by basil and mint leaves.

Ingredients for one pizza

Pizza dough → PAGE 75 .... 5 oz / 150 g
Herb-infused oil → BELOW .... 1½ tsp
plus extra for drizzling
Prosciutto crudo, sliced .... 2 oz / 60 g
Fabula cheese .... 1 oz / 30 g
Cilento white fig jam .... ¾ oz / 25 g
Fresh mint leaves 3
Fresh basil leaves 2

Ingredients for the herb-infused oil

Extra virgin olive oil .... 10 fl oz / 300 ml
Sprigs of Mediterranean herbs (thyme, oregano)

Pitta Fabula → IMAGE PAGE 190

To make the herb-infused oil, combine the oil with the oregano and thyme sprigs in a bowl and let steep for 6 hours. Strain to remove the herbs, and store in an airtight container.
Stretch the dough into a disk without creating a crust.
Drizzle with 1½ teaspoons of infused oil and bake for 1 minute 30 seconds at 790–840°F / 420–450°C.
Once cooked, fold in half to create a pocket, and fill the pocket with prosciutto, Fabula cheese, fig jam, mint leaves, basil leaves, and another drizzle of infused oil.

Pitta Stufata

During the Covid-19 pandemic, when everything came to a standstill in Italy, work at the Pepe in Grani pizzeria did not stop; instead, pizza delivery became a mission. And because the pizzas were delivered not only in Caiazzo but also to many neighboring cities and towns, the idea of making *pitte*, folded and stuffed pizzas, was born. They are easy to make and reheat, and they are delicious, even though the pizza is not freshly baked.

Pitta Stufata has very simple ingredients, reminiscent of the Pepe family's tradition of baking endive (frisée) pizza for lunch on Christmas Eve while preparing the Christmas dinner celebrated that night. Because it was important to have dinner on an empty stomach, it was the only other meal allowed that day. This folded pizza is filled with a wonderful preparation that is typical of the rural tradition of Campania.

Ingredients for one pizza

Pizza dough → PAGE 75 .... 5 oz / 150 g
Stewed endive → BELOW .... 7 oz / 200 g
Smoked provola cheese, sliced .... 1 oz / 30 g
Herb-infused oil → PAGE 189 .... 1½ tsp

Ingredients for the stewed endive

Extra virgin olive oil .... 1½ tsp
Cetara anchovy fillets .... ¾ oz / 20 g
Dried capers .... ¼ oz / 8 g
Curly endive (frisée) .... 3½ oz / 100 g
Pine nuts .... ½ oz / 15 g
Golden raisins (sultanas) .... ¾ oz / 20 g
Prunes .... ¾ oz / 20 g
Annurca apple .... 1 (about 5 oz / 150 g)

Pitta Stufata → IMAGE PAGE 191

For the stewed endive, heat a little oil in a skillet (frying pan) and sauté the anchovies and capers for 5 minutes. Tear the endive (frisée) with your hands and add to the skillet, together with the pine nuts, golden raisins (sultanas), prunes, and the apple cut into ½-inch / 1-cm dice. Cover and cook, about 20 minutes.

Stretch the dough into a disk without creating a crust.

Drizzle with a little of the herb-infused oil, and bake for 1 minute 30 seconds at 790–840°F / 420–450°C. Then add the stewed endive and sliced cheese. Drizzle with the remaining infused oil, fold, and bake for another 20 seconds.

Sciuccaglia

Unlike other breeds, Black Casertano pigs develop a wattle, known locally as a *sciuccaglia*, that hangs from their jowls like a pendant of skin. For this reason, the pigs themselves are given this name, considered a tongue twister in the local dialect.

This pizza was invented as Covid-19 began and was made with the few preserved ingredients left in the pizzeria's refrigerators and store rooms, with guanciale as the predominant flavor. It is combined with the sweetness of a purée made of sautéed onions, the delicious flavor of sun-dried tomatoes, and the intensity of Matese oregano.

Maialino nero Casertano (Black Casertano pigs).

Above: Guanciale curing.
Opposite: Guanciale, pancetta, and more cure on racks.

Ingredients for one pizza

Pizza dough → PAGE 75 . . . . **10 oz / 280 g**
Alife onions, julienned . . . . **3 oz / 90 g**
Sun-dried San Marzano tomatoes in oil . . . . **2 3/4 oz / 80 g**
Oil from the sun-dried tomatoes . . . . **2 tsp**
Casertano pork guanciale (cured pork cheek), thinly sliced . . . . **2 oz / 60 g**
Matese oregano, dried . . . . **generous 2 tsp / 5 g**

Sciuccaglia

Stretch the dough into a disk, leaving a uniform crust around the entire circumference.
Top with the onion and the sun-dried tomatoes and their oil, and bake for 1 minute 30 seconds–2 minutes at 790–840°F / 420–450°C.
Once cooked, add the guanciale slices and sprinkle with the oregano.

Nero Fumè

Hay is set alight to smoke mozzarella and make scamorza.

"For a long time, I wanted the Pepe in Grani menu to include a pizza base made with a smoked *fior di latte* cheese," says Franco Pepe. "That's how, together with the Sorì Dairy and after two years of planning, we came up with a *fior di latte* (both smoked and plain) made from the milk of buffaloes reared two miles (three kilometers) away from the pizzeria, in the mountains of Matese and Fortore, and ripened in the volcanic spring water of Roccamonfina: Fior di Latte Appennino Campano."

On the pizza, the wood smoke notes of the *fior di latte* cheese are accompanied by the smoky aroma and intensity of cellar-cured sausage.

Freshly smoked scamorza cools.

Ingredients for one pizza

Pizza dough → PAGE 75 .... **10 oz / 280 g**
Smoked fior di latte (cow's milk mozzarella), sliced .... **5 oz / 150 g**
Cured Casertana pork sausage, thinly sliced .... **2 1/2 oz / 70 g**
Extra virgin olive oil .... **1 1/2 tsp**
plus extra for drizzling
Cherry tomato confit in extra virgin olive oil .... **1 1/2 oz / 40 g**

Nero Fumè

Stretch the dough ball into a disk, leaving a uniform crust around the entire circumference.

Top with slices of smoked fior di latte cheese and cured sausage. Drizzle with the 1½ teaspoons of oil, and bake for 1 minute 30 seconds–2 minutes at 790–840°F / 420–450°C.

Once cooked, add the tomato confit and drizzle with more extra virgin olive oil.

Alletterata

The whole of Campania is reflected in this pizza, from the back country to the coast, from the Alife onion and Mozzarella di Bufala, to the sea and its fish. The absolute star is the little tunny, a Mediterranean tuna that has spots on its back that look like irregular black drawings, almost like letters and symbols (hence the Italian name *alletterato*, "lettered"). Typically packed in oil, this delicate tuna, in combination with extremely sweet onion and crisp celery curls, makes for a beautifully balanced pizza.

ngredients for one pizza

izza dough → PAGE 75 .... **10 oz / 280 g**
elery stalk .... **2 oz / 60 g**
life onion purée → PAGE 133 .... **2 1/2 oz / 70 g**
ozzarella di Bufala di Campania PDO, sliced .... **3 1/2 oz / 100 g**
xtra virgin olive oil .... **1 1/2 tsp**
ittle tuna fillets in oil .... **2 3/4 oz / 80 g**

Alletterata → IMAGE PAGE 206

Wash the celery, remove the strings, and cut into very thin strips lengthwise. Place in plenty of ice water to curl.

Stretch the dough ball into a disk, leaving a uniform crust around the entire circumference.

Spread with the onion purée and add the mozzarella slices. Then drizzle with oil and bake for 1 minute 30 seconds–2 minutcs at 790–840°F / 420–450°C. Once cooked, complete the topping with tuna and celery curls.

Aglio Olio e Peperoncino

There is more to this pizza than meets the eye. Despite its very plain appearance, it amazes with its explosion of flavors and contrasts. The popularity of *spaghetti ajio e olio* (with garlic and oil) is also confirmed in tribute to the dish, which after baking is enhanced with anchovies and the freshness of parsley.

Ingredients for one pizza

- **Pizza dough** → PAGE 75 .... **10 oz / 280 g**
- **Black Casertano pig lardo** .... **1 tsp / 5 g**
- **Chopped chili pepper** .... **1 tsp / 3 g**
- **Garlic, chopped** .... **1 clove**
- **Extra virgin olive oil** .... **1½ tsp**
- **Cetara anchovy fillets** .... **2 oz / 60 g**
- **Fresh parsley, chopped** .... **⅓ oz / 10 g**

Aglio Olio e Peperoncino → IMAGE PAGE 207

Stretch the dough ball into a disk, leaving a uniform crust around the entire circumference.

Top with the lardo, chili pepper, and garlic. Then drizzle with the oil and bake for 1 minute 30 seconds at 790 840°F / 420–450°C.

Once cooked, add the anchovy fillets and chopped parsley.

Mangiabufala

This pizza features three gastronomic masterpieces produced by three of Franco Pepe's close friends: Mimmo La Vecchia, with his incredible bloomy rind cheese; Armando De Nigris, with his intense balsamic vinegar; and Raffaele Garofalo, with his aromatic buffalo bresaola. These ingredients come together in a very interesting harmony of flavors on the pizza.

Fabula is a buffalo cheese that disproves the belief that only mozzarella can be made from buffalo milk. After aging about 30 days and forming a bloomy rind, the cheese becomes creamy and intense. On the pizza it replaces mozzarella and melts to add body and a delicate flavor. The locally produced bresaola, cured buffalo meat, is very aromatic and intensifies and adds complexity to the flavor of the pizza when added after cooking. Finally, croutons seasoned with De Nigris Balsamic Vinegar of Modena PGI are added for both crispness and notes of sweet and sour.

As Franco Pepe explains, "A pizza that was invented for fun, inspired by the classic carpaccio seasoned with balsamic vinegar, turned into a really good Italian pizza: intense, fresh, and balsamic."

Mimmo La Vecchia, owner and cheese maker at Caseficio Il Casolare. The La Vecchia family has been producing Mozzarella Campana PDO and a wide range of dairy products for three generations in a dairy farm near Alvignano, in the province of Caserta.

Above: Balls of mozzarella hit the salt water bath.
Opposite: Cheesemakers at Caseficio Il Casolare pull mozzarella di bufala.

Ingredients for one pizza

Pizza dough → PAGE 75 .... **10 oz / 280 g**
Cream cheese (made with Fabula cheese) → PAGE 122 ....
4 1/4 oz / 120 g
Fior di latte (cow's milk mozzarella), sliced .. **2 oz / 60 g**
Extra virgin olive oil .... **1 1/2 tsp**
Buffalo bresaola, julienned .... **2 oz / 60 g**
Curly endive (frisée) .... **3/4 oz / 20 g**
Chopped walnuts .... **3/4 oz / 20 g**

Ingredients for the balsamic vinegar croutons

Pane casereccio (Italian rustic bread) .... **1/2 oz / 15 g**
Balsamic Vinegar of Modena PGI .... **1 1/4 tsp**

Mangiabufala

To make the balsamic vinegar croutons, simply cut the bread into ½-inch / 1-cm chunks, toast the chunks in a nonstick pan until crispy. Set aside.

Stretch the dough into a disk, leaving a uniform crust around the entire circumference.

Spread with the cheese cream (any left over will keep in the refrigerator for 2–3 days), add the fior di latte cheese, drizzle with oil, and bake for 1 minute 30 seconds–2 minutes at 790–840°F / 420–450°C.

While the pizza is cooking, drizzle the croutons with the balsamic vinegar. It is important to only do this as the pizza is baking to prevent them from becoming soggy.

Once cooked, top with the bresaola, hand-torn endive (frisée), walnuts, and balsamic vinegar croutons.

Gelsomina

Succo di gelsi (mulberry juice) is a rare product from a rare fruit. But if you are lucky enough to have or to find a mulberry tree in the summer when the berries are very ripe, blend and strain them to make this deep-colored, sweet liquid whose flavor is reminiscent of blackberries and fruits of the forest.

"This pizza was invented one day when our regular delivery of Vesuvius apricot compote arrived at Pepe in Grani with a bottle of a delicious juice with an amazing purple color. We immediately made it into a syrup, and then a pizza that we dedicated to my mother's mother, Gelsomina," Franco says.

This deep-fried pizza is a burst of flavor, creaminess, and color, with the richness of the pastry cream and fresh notes from the syrup.

Ingredients for one pizza

Pizza dough → PAGE 75 .... **7 oz / 200 g**
Pastry cream → PAGE 219 .... **3 1/2 oz / 100 g**
Unsalted butter .... **1/3 oz / 10 g**
Mulberry syrup .... **2 oz / 60 g**
Violet crystals .... **1/2 oz / 15 g**
Confectioners' (icing) sugar .... **1/3 oz / 10 g**
Lime zest, grated .... **1/2 tsp / 2 g**
Sunflower oil, for deep-frying

Gelsomina

Stretch the dough ball into a disk and prick all over with a fork. Heat plenty of sunflower oil in a large pan to 410–430°F / 210–220°C, and deep-fry the pizza for about 1 minute, until golden.

Once cooked, cut the disk into 4 slices. Place a knob of butter on each slice and distribute the pastry cream using a pastry (piping) bag. Using a squeeze bottle, add the mulberry syrup, then sprinkle over the violet crystals and confectioners' (icing) sugar, and finish with the lime zest.

Ingredients for the pastry cream

Fresh milk	1 cup / 250 ml
Lemon zest	generous 2 tsp / 5 g
Granulated sugar	3 oz / 80 g
Pasteurized egg yolks	1 3/4 oz / 40 g
Whole egg	1
Italian type 00 flour, sifted	3/4 oz / 20 g

Pastry cream

For the pastry cream, heat the milk in a saucepan with the lemon zest.
In a bowl, whisk the sugar with the egg yolks and whole egg, then gradually incorporate the sifted flour to create a smooth cream.
When the milk reaches 203°F / 95°C, add the milk to the bowl. Whisk vigorously until smooth. Place the mixture over a pan of simmering water to create a bain-marie, while stirring with the whisk to the desired consistency.
When the pastry cream is ready, cover with plastic wrap (cling film) and let cool. Transfer the pastry cream to a pastry (piping) bag and refrigerate for at least 3 hours. Use within 1 day.

Cerasella

This pizza is entirely the work of Franco's son, Stefano. By melding memories with creativity, he devised a sweet pizza with a savory contrast in the form of salt flakes, in addition to alcohol and an interesting variation of temperatures that enhance its intense freshness. This pizza is dedicated to his grandmother, Gaetana, the mother of his mother Rita, with whom he was raised. "I used to spend a lot of time with her in the kitchen," Stefano recalls. "I think that's where my passion for cooking came from. One day I went to Grandma Gaetana's house for a coffee before heading to work at the pizzeria. Grandma was putting *cerase* (cherries) in brandy to preserve them. I stole a jar of her brandied cherries and ran to the pizzeria to experiment with a pizza. At first the *pizzaioli* didn't understand what I was doing when they saw me injecting alcohol into the pizza with a syringe, but as soon as they tasted it, they knew I was right. This pizza went onto the menu that very evening and has been one of our bestselling desserts ever since."

Stefano puts the finishing touches to a Cerasella pizza at Pepe in Grani.

Ingredients for one pizza

Pizza dough → PAGE 75 .... **7 oz / 200 g**
Fior di latte flakes → BELOW .... **4 oz / 120 g**
Falernum liqueur .... **2 tsp**
Dark chocolate, 70% .... **1 oz / 30 g**
Maldon sea salt flakes .... **to taste**
Fresh mint leaves **6**
Orange zest, grated .... **to taste**
Brandied cherries **6**
Sunflower oil, for deep-frying

Ingredients for the fior di latte flakes

Cooking cream .... **3 ½ oz / 100 g**
Granulated sugar .... **¾ oz / 20 g**
Fior di latte (cow's milk mozzarella) .... **1¾ oz / 50 g**
Orange zest, grated .... **to taste**

Cerasella

For the fior di latte flakes, pour the cream into a saucepan and bring to a boil, stirring constantly. Once it comes to a boil, add the sugar, stir, and pour it into a blender and add the fior di latte and orange zest. Blend everything for 10 seconds, then spread the mixture on a baking sheet lined with baking parchment to create a thin sheet, and place it in the freezer. Once the sheet has cooled, it can be used.
Stretch the dough into a disk. Heat plenty of sunflower oil in a large pan to 410–430°F / 210–220°C, and deep-fry the pizza for about 1 minute, until golden.
Once cooked, cut the disk into 6 slices and use a syringe to inject each slice with ½ teaspoon of liqueur.
Place the chocolate in a heatproof bowl set over a small saucepan of simmering water to create a bain-marie, then allow to melt.
Arrange frozen fior di latte flakes on each slice of pizza, drizzle over the melted chocolate, add the salt flakes and mint, and sprinkle over the orange zest. Serve each slice with a brandied cherry.

PEPE GRANI
PEPE IN I
225

A Different Kind of Pizzeria

The moment Pepe in Grani opened, its customers understood that this was a very different kind of pizzeria, one that was totally out of the ordinary.

The first thing that customers appreciated was the overall quality of the food. The meticulously handmade dough meant that Pepe in Grani pizzas not only had a strong aroma of wheat, but were very light, almost melting on the palate, with clear, precise flavors and a perfect style of cooking.

Franco used the months while the restaurant was being constructed to strengthen his relationships with local producers, so that the pizzas could be created using only the outstanding products of the Caiazzo region. Many of these excellent local ingredients were in danger of disappearing: by choosing them for use in his pizzas he helped to reclaim and relaunch them.

The search for produce clearly set out the sustainability of the Pepe in Grani project, dedicated to the recovery of ancient varieties of cereals, legumes, and plants, the re-evaluation of longstanding rural expertise that was progressively being lost, and collaboration and trust with the modern guardians of a farming economy that was primarily local. Each pizza brought together these sensitivities, along with an exceptional human and entrepreneurial commitment.

The Pepe in Grani project has been based on a strong blueprint from the outset, providing a multisensory experience for diners, in which the full story of each pizza is told through design, images, words, and flavors. This is a pizzeria based on the spirit of fine

Page 224: Franco with his young son, Stefano.

dining, offering the quality and service of a great restaurant—with a wine list of over 140 labels—but above all delivering a series of pizza tastings conceived as individual courses: a pizza "tasting menu." From the beginning the tasting menu has always started with a fried pizza, moving on to several slices of savory pizza (four, five, or eight pieces, depending on the menu chosen), and ending with sweet fried pizza. A typical table of six diners can therefore enjoy a good selection of Pepe in Grani's iconic pizzas, tasting a slice of each.

This was the first time that the pizza experience had been transformed into a tasting menu. Pizza, by tradition, was eaten alone, perhaps preceded by some fried delicacies. On Pepe in Grani's menu, however, "pizza" has become a collective noun, describing a diverse experience that takes the diner on a journey through the various stages of an intense, carefully planned meal intended to evoke powerful feelings of emotion and pleasure. Even the design of the accessories—the plates and the methods of enjoying pizza (whether with cutlery or hands)—has been carefully studied, taking the diner ever closer to an elegant, finely tuned, high-end dining experience, while retaining the down-to-earth essence of pizza consumption with traditional materials such as wood and copper.

Dining at Pepe in Grani has continued to evolve over the years into an increasingly nuanced, immersive, and tech-savvy experience. In 2015 a new room was created on the first floor, comprising just three round tables whose glass surfaces incorporate a central lens in which each new pizza is placed. Video images of pizza production are shown at two of the tables, but the third faces directly onto a hatch positioned opposite the second oven—added to the kitchens more recently to speed up the process—allowing the diners at this table to observe the pizza chefs at work. In addition, rooms on the building's top floor were transformed into hotel accommodation. Even the idea of customers staying overnight in rooms in the same building was a small revolution, bringing Pepe in Grani closer to the classic French tradition of *grandes tables,* with total 360-degree hospitality: a "pizzeria with rooms."

Yet the large turnover at the restaurant, and the growing number of diners, began to give Franco the feeling that he was steadily losing contact with his customers, and he became increasingly concerned by the need to rediscover the "human factor" that tends to be more difficult to maintain as numbers grow. It was precisely in order to bridge this growing distance that "Authentica" was created—a small room on the top floor incorporating a third oven placed in front of a curved table, where Franco can welcome groups of no more than eight. Authentica opened in 2017, but it truly represents the future, since this new dining format was the first time that a pizzeria had placed guests in direct contact with the pizza chef, allowing diners to talk directly with the chef in a situation of unique intimacy and interchange. This is a dining style based on the ideas of exclusivity, rarity, and desire, which have more to do with pure luxury and high quality than the popular, widespread views of a classic pizzeria. Over time, Authentica has also become a room of great innovation and improvisation, with a calendar of special events involving famous chefs, pastry chefs, and restaurateurs from all over the world. These became sought-after events for the very few, in which new recipes, ideas, and collaborations could be conceived.

Sunset from a window of Pepe in Grani.

Without the participation of a great team, the Pepe in Grani format would never have evolved into the harmonious system that it is today. Constantly passing on his knowledge to his children, Francesca and Stefano, and all of the staff, Franco Pepe has built an organic system of research, innovation, hospitality, communication, dining room, and kitchen. From washing to wine service, from hospitality to the cash register, from marketing to communication, from producers and ingredients to the pizza on the plate—everything is done with style and elegance.

Pepe in Grani was created exactly as it had appeared in Franco's dream: "a high-end pizzeria with a down-to-earth soul," founded on a mix of balances that made the difference from the beginning of the customer experience, a set of details that made everything unique.

The fourth pillar on which the Pepe in Grani project is based, in addition to quality, the dining format, and the team, is its strong ongoing awareness of health. From the very beginning, Franco Pepe included an agronomist, Vincenzo Coppola, and a nutritionist, Michelina Petrazzuoli, in his team.

"I needed to have science by my side, because as well as making a great pizza purely for its deliciousness, I also wanted to make the perfect pizza from the point of view of health and environmental issues," explains Franco.

This partnership with an agronomist has guaranteed the seasonality of the vegetables and agricultural products used at Pepe in Grani, as well as the quality of ancient varieties in danger of extinction. It also meant that there was a coherent, planned program of agricultural crops, and real concrete assistance was provided to all the farmers with whom Franco collaborated. It was possible to guarantee not only that the restaurant was using excellent, healthy, natural products, but also that the food produced at Pepe in Grani was fully sustainable, with low environmental impact and a totally controlled supply chain.

As a result of the research carried out with the nutritionist Petrazzuoli, it soon became clear that, thanks to fundamental attention to the ingredients (which were all as untreated and natural as possible), the cooking and temperatures (not too high and differentiated), and, above all, the combinations and quantities of ingredients, it was possible to offer the public an even healthier pizza, the consumption of which was no longer "rule-breaking," but could even be regarded as a positive dietary habit.

This research led to the creation of a section of the Pepe in Grani menu dedicated purely to "Mediterranean pizza," comprising slightly smaller pizzas (7 oz / 200 g instead of 9 oz / 250 g) accompanied by raw vegetables (wild chicory, chard, borage, "artichoke thistles," wild arugula [rocket], and torzella cabbage), and a dressing in which to dunk the crust. This is a healthy menu based on the idea of a pizza achieving the right balance of macronutrients (namely carbohydrates, proteins, and fats), combined with sauces and vegetables, guaranteeing the ideal caloric intake of 55–60 percent carbohydrates, 15–20 percent proteins, and 25–30 percent fats, according to the "food pyramid" of the classic Mediterranean diet, and including the ideal proportions of fiber, antioxidants, and mineral salts.

Since then, the menu at Pepe in Grani has always included a selection of pizzas accompanied by raw vegetables. These increase the fiber content of the dish, balance the glycemic load of the meal, speed up digestion, and balance the assimilation and elimination of fats.

The people of Caiazzo and the surrounding province have all welcomed Franco Pepe. Even the Neapolitans, despite an initial wariness, have begun to frequent Pepe in Grani. Once the restaurant had been highlighted by gastronomic guides (its first Tre Spicchi award in the *Gambera Rosso Pizzerie d'Italia* guide came in 2013), the queues ran along the slope of the alley, growing longer day by day, and began to include many customers from Rome and the north.

The first unexpected explosion of success, on a scale absolutely beyond any prediction, occurred nearly two years after Pepe in Grani opened. One evening, Faith Willinger, an American journalist and writer who had been based in Italy for many years, gave Franco a friendly call to tell him that among the customers in the dining room of his pizzeria was none other than Jonathan Gold, the renowned "Poet of the Palate" and the first food critic to have won the Pulitzer Prize. Soon afterwards, an article appeared in *Food & Wine USA* magazine under Gold's name, headed: "This might be the greatest pizza in the world." Gold had been tipped off about the opening of this pizzeria in the upper Caserta area by Nancy Silverton, a well-known American chef who owns the Mozza pizzerias in Los Angeles and Newport. They met after Nancy returned from a vacation in Italy where she had been to Caiazzo, and she passed on her thoughts on pizza to Gold: "I've never had pizza in Naples that I've liked. But if I'd known about Franco Pepe before I opened Mozza, I probably wouldn't have made pizza at all. People have been making it for hundreds of years in Campania, but it feels almost as if Franco just invented pizza and everyone else is copying him. It's like those chefs who started doing 'molecular gastronomy' after they saw what Ferran Adrià was doing at El Bulli.

ranco Pepe with Brian McGinn, Executive Producer/Director
f Netflix's *Chef's Table*

It's kind of hard to explain, but Franco has this glow around him. His is probably the best pizza in the world."

In 2015 Nancy Silverton returned to Caiazzo to shoot a TV show with Emeril Lagasse: *Eat the World with Emeril Lagasse.* Franco Pepe was yet again feted as the best pizza chef in the world, and became their guide on a fascinating televisual journey through gastronomic Campania, steering his way through a variety of kitchens, producers, and restaurants.

After this first exposure on TV, numerous international customers began to arrive in Caiazzo. Many had come in previous years thanks to a banging of the culinary gong by military staff in the NATO command center at Naples. However, the response to Nancy Silverton created an even more powerful and unstoppable buzz around Pepe in Grani. The next TV event was an episode of the Netflix series *Ugly Delicious,* presented by David Chang in 2018. This was a convivial discussion on food, highlighting the many different players in the pizza sector: from the True Neapolitan Pizza Association to Susumu Kakinuma (the pizza chef of Seirinkan restaurant in Tokyo), and from Domino's Pizza in the USA to Pepe in Grani in Caiazzo.

Nothing, however, can quite compare with the success that followed in 2022, with the broadcasting of a pizza-oriented episode of *Chef's Table* (a Netflix series created by David Gelb and directed by Brian McGinn), which focused specifically on Franco Pepe. This documentary was narrated by Franco's friend Faith Willinger, and with it he achieved the highest possible media profile. The queue in the *vicolo* became increasingly international, varied, and lengthy. In addition to the real queue in front of the pizzeria, the waiting list to get a table also grew, and the restaurant reached truly impressive numbers of customers and orders, often exceeding a thousand pizzas per evening. Resisting the temptation to simply ride the wave, Franco deliberately tried not to overdo the number of covers, so that the quality of the food served to customers from all over the world could be maintained.

After a succession of awards and conferences, Franco Pepe and Pepe in Grani have now become a constant and unshakable feature of international cuisine, but, despite the increased recognition, the restaurant's fundamental path and direction remain the same.

In 2016, Franco attracted the highest numbers of votes for a pizza chef in the guide *Where to Eat Pizza,* edited by Daniel Young and published by Phaidon: Pepe in Grani was voted top international pizzeria by over a thousand experts called to give their opinion on where they had eaten the best pizza in the world.

And over the last fourteen years, Franco Pepe has featured repeatedly at Identità Golose, the major Italian cuisine congress, created by Paolo Marchi in 2004. Franco has honorably demonstrated that pizza does not have to be in a separate room at conferences, but can feature proudly on the main stage together with the great chefs and cuisines of the world.

Pepe in Grani has been at the top of the rankings in all Italian food and restaurant guides for years, and Franco Pepe himself has received many important awards at an international level. In 2019,

Pepe in Grani was the first pizzeria in the world to be included in the "50 Best Discovery" ranking. And in 2024, after four consecutive years recognized as "best pizza in the world," Franco Pepe was given the prestigious "2 Knives" award at the Best Chef Awards in Dubai, becoming the first and only pizza chef to receive it.

The awards that most excite Franco Pepe, however, are the two Knighthoods of Merit of the Italian Republic (for his commitment to the Campanian region and for his volunteer work during the Covid 19 pandemic) awarded by the President, Sergio Mattarella; and the "Master of the Art of Italian Cuisine," a unique recognition that rewards creativity and entrepreneurship in the Italian gastronomic panorama, received in April 2025. These awards represent the first time in the history of the Italian Republic that a pizza chef had been awarded such important honors.

"All these awards embarrass me," says Franco. "In twelve years of Pepe in Grani, without these awards I would not have been able to do what I did. I would be a hypocrite if I said otherwise. What these awards and documentaries have also made possible is the strengthening of my great team (we started off as just seven, and today there are fifty of us), the growth of my children Francesca and Stefano alongside me, and the development of the local economy in a way that no one could have imagined."

In fact, from 2012 onwards, a whole new world of tourism has been brought to Caiazzo by Franco Pepe, along with an entire economic chain. Dozens of B&Bs, accommodation facilities, and dedicated travel agencies have been created to organize walks, delightful explorations of the surrounding region, and visits to the many rural and artisan operations that today make up the Pepe in Grani universe. Around Franco an entire city has grown—a whole new human, economic, and social network.

The Future

Franco Pepe has achieved important goals, and he can now afford to digest everything with the awareness of someone who started from the bottom and ended up creating something totally unique.

His aim for the next ten years is to pass on his legacy of pizza expertise to his children and the whole Pepe in Grani team. He dreams of further projects that will involve young people without a future, including collaborations with various volunteer associations. Certainly, his work has already begun to create a cultural education around the idea of good, healthy pizza, referring to pizza that is creative and innovative, "outside the box," personal and unique, always kneaded by hand, and made according to a recipe that is both ancient and new. This has been a revolutionary path, leaving an indelible mark on the world of pizza, not just the Neapolitan variety but throughout the world. This simultaneously ancient and contemporary "round trip" is not an impossible oxymoron, but a concrete project that has essentially been realized. It is a visionary dream that has actually come true, and it is still emerging today, through research and innovation, yet never forgetting its roots, the lessons learned along the way, and what is the right legacy to carry forward.

Now is the time to focus on education and the transmission of knowledge. Francesca and Stefano are like two sponges, absorbing and metabolizing the important messages that they receive daily. Francesca is focused on communication, strategy, and the sheer "elegance" of the project. Decisive and determined, she tells the story of the emergence of Pepe in Grani with consummate passion and style. Stefano is the "oil" keeping the cogs of the company turning with his coordination of the team and his designs for new pizzas and projects, working alongside his father. Both have beautiful eyes, like their grandfather, and they never stop using them to visualize the many future projects that are still in their early stages.

Vicolo S. Giovanni Battista is a long alleyway, and while we may close the pages on the current book, new projects are already leavening, new receptacles for dreams yet undreamed, inexorably rising like the dough in Pepe in Grani.

Stefano, Franco, and Francesca Pepe.

INDEX

CAIAZZO
1
50

Phaidon Press Limited
2 Cooperage Yard
London E15 2QR

Phaidon Press Inc.
111 Broadway
New York, NY 10006

Phaidon SARL
55, rue Traversière
75012 Paris

phaidon.com

First published 2025

ISBN 978 1 83729 061 1

A CIP catalogue record for this book is available from the British Library and the Library of Congress.

Commissioning Editor: Emilia Terragni
Project Editor: Rachel Malig
Designer: Studio Mut, Anni Seligmann & Martin Kerschbaumer
Production Controller: Rebecca Price
Photography: Adam Bricker and Brian McGinn

Printed in China

The publisher would like to thank Vanessa Bird, Bret Curry, Jack Devanna, Nathan Kellum, Leica Camera, João Mota, Ellie Smith, Tracey Smith, and Kathy Steer for their contributions to the book.

Acknowledgments

Franco Pepe would like to extend his heartfelt thanks, first and foremost, to Stefano Pepe, Francesca Pepe, and Carolina Pepe for their important contribution to the creation of this project. Special thanks also go to the entire team at Pepe in Grani, to author Elisia Menduni, and to photographers Brian McGinn and Adam Bricker for their valuable collaboration and deep synergy.

He would also like to express his gratitude for the kind participation of: Nancy Silverton, Faith Willinger, Daniel Young, Luigi Cremona, Carla Capalbo, the I Love Matese association, the Lombardi Family from Agriturismo Le Campestre, the Sangiovanni Family from Azienda Sangiovanni, the La Vecchia Family from Il Casolare, Azienda Agricola Antonietta Melillo, La Sbecciatrice, Tomaso Salumi, Molino Piantoni, Azienda Agricola Ammendola, Francesco Palladino, architect Beniamino Di Fusco, Filippo Petraglia, Professor Ortensio Marcucci, Massimiliano Pepe, and Nicola Santacroce.

About the authors

Franco Pepe learned his trade from his grandparents, parents, and siblings, and also from time spent among the pizza masters of Naples. He set up Pepe in Grani in Caiazzo to follow his own vision and, since then, he has won countless awards, including Knight of the Order of Merit of the Italian Republic in 2019 and 2020. His pizza and his pizzeria are constantly ranked the best in the world.

Elisia Menduni is an anthropologist, pizza and baking expert, food writer, food creative, and independent scholar. She is known for her writing, reporting, photography, and video making.

Recipe notes

Butter should always be unsalted, unless otherwise specified.

All herbs are fresh, unless otherwise specified.

Eggs are medium (US large) unless otherwise specified.

Individual vegetables and fruits, such as onions and apples, are assumed to be medium, unless otherwise specified.

All milk is whole (3% fat), homogenized, and lightly pasteurized, unless otherwise specified.

All salt is fine salt, unless otherwise specified.

Exercise a high level of caution when following recipes involving any potentially hazardous activity, including the use of high temperatures, open flames, and when deep-frying. In particular, when deep-frying add food carefully to avoid splashing, wear long sleeves and never leave the pan unattended.

Cooking times are for guidance only. If using a fan (convection) oven, follow the manufacturer's instructions concerning the oven temperatures.

All herbs, shoots, flowers, and leaves should be picked fresh from a clean source. Do exercise caution when foraging for ingredients, which should only be eaten if an expert has deemed them safe to eat. In particular, do not gather wild mushrooms yourself before seeking the advice of an expert who has confirmed their suitability for human consumption. As some species of mushrooms have been known to cause allergic reaction and illness, do take extra care when cooking and eating mushrooms and do seek immediate medical help if you experience a reaction after preparing or eating them.

Exercise caution when making fermented products, ensuring all equipment is spotlessly clean, and seek expert advice if in any doubt.

When no quantity is specified, for example of oils, salts, and herbs used for finishing dishes, quantities are discretionary and flexible.

All spoon and cup measurements are level, unless otherwise stated. 1 teaspoon = 5 ml; 1 tablespoon = 15 ml. Australian standard tablespoons are 20 ml, so Australian readers are advised to use 3 teaspoons in place of 1 tablespoon when measuring small quantities.

Cup, metric, and imperial measurements are used in this book. Follow one set of measurements throughout, not a mixture, as they are not interchangeable.